1

Testimonials

"Cory Mosley is among the best trainers in the business today. His 'new school' approach to developing sales strategies is spot on. I had the good fortune to work with Cory on the development of a training course for an OEM which was very successful. I am looking forward to our next opportunity to collaborate on a project." - **Daniel Hill, Account Manager: Alteris Group**

"With thousands of dealerships using our CRM software, we are big believers in training and processes. I have known Cory for years now and he is a great asset to all the dealerships we work together on. After analyzing the strengths and areas of opportunity with in a department, he creates tailored processes and a training curriculum to improve these areas. I endorse Cory Mosley, but his track record speaks for itself." - **Matt Redden, EVP: Dealersocket CRM**

The Way I See It

Thoughts, Commentary, and Musings of a Retail Car Guy

Cory Mosley

The Way I See It
Thoughts, Commentary, and Musings of a Retail Car Guy
Author: Cory Mosley
Published by: Mosley Automotive Press
3741 Westerre Parkway Suite B
Richmond, VA 23233

www.mosleyautomotive.com

For bulk book purchasing, please contact Xiomara Mosley
at: Tel: 877-667-5398
Email: info@mosleytraining.com

This book is dedicated to the industry that has allowed me to provide for myself and for my family for the past 16 years, the auto industry.

CLM

Disclaimer

Foreword

Thirty-eight years in the retail automobile industry, I've reached the top of my game, been a long-running featured columnist in some of the most read national industry publications, spoken at more than one hundred state and national dealer conventions and I've set records in the retail industry. Suffice it to say I am not easily impressed with the 'New Age' writers, trainers and consultants emerging in our industry and clamoring for status and recognition.

Back in 2005, I was a featured speaker at one of the early Digital Dealer Conferences. There was a lot of Buzz about the 'New Kid' speaking, consulting and writing about the retail car business. From the very first time I saw him and listened to his message, I knew Cory Mosley was a winner destined to make a meaningful impact in the evolution of our business and processes. Everyone knew he was going places.

Unlike so many other next generation speakers and trainers, Cory is a visionary who is still firmly anchored in the reality of the real-world car business. In short; the man gets it.

In those years since we first met, we've become friends. I hold Cory in high regard and he has been a featured, main-stage speaker at five of my Internet Battle Plan Conferences.

Cory Mosley: We've written for the same magazines, spoken at the same conventions and conferences, both members of the National Speakers Association, and we've crossed paths many times in the retail arena as we both travel around the country helping dealerships realize ultimate sales and profitability. Our families have traveled and socialized together, and we share insights regularly.

This compilation of Cory Mosley's techniques and philosophies will indelibly imprint these valuable concepts into your dealership's business disciplines and regimens. I'll be the very first to read it myself.

JIM ZIEGLER, CSP, HSG

Acknowledgements

Thank you to the following individuals who without their contributions and support this book would not have been written:

Greg Arroyo

Tariq Kamal

The Team at Bobit Business Media

My wife, Xiomara Mosley

Fellow writer Jim "the alpha dawg" Ziegler

Ronn Stern for the great artwork

Dementi Studios

My 2014 Motivation Committee
(Sean V. Bradley, Paul Potratz, and Grant Cardone)

All the dealerships around the country that I get to visit.

Table of Contents

Introduction 13

    Salesperson 14

    Sales Manager...14

    Dealer Principal 15

I Sales and Selling 18

  1. Sweat the Small Stuff...19

    Real Life Is the Best Teacher 20

    Small Things Become Big Things 21

    Self-Assess...21

  2. Challenge Yourself 23

  3. Showroom Confidential 27

  4. Hunter to Influencer 31

    The Return of Authenticity....................................32

    Gaining Influence 33

  5. Becoming Influential...35

6. Execution Plan 39

7. The 'New' Road to a Sale 43

8. Self-Sabotaging Behaviors to Avoid 47

9. The Four 'Cs' of Phone Prospecting 53

10. Six Sales-Driving Ideas...............................58

11. It's in the Presentation...............................62

12. A Basic Problem 66

II. Sales Management 71

13. Signing Rookies 72

14. The Gross Killer 76

15.   4.5 Success Drivers 80

16. Dead or Alive?...85

17. Three Traffic Drivers 89

18. Pay It Forward...93

19. It's OK to 'Think Different' 97

Training and Development.............................97

Cleaning House 99

20. Challenging the Status Quo 101

Problem 1: The Work Schedule.....................102

Problem No. 2: Managers vs. Leaders.........103

21. No Training, No Complaining 106

22. Momentum: Getting It and Keeping It 110

23. Four Operational Game-Changers 114

24. Seven Team-Building Must-Haves 118

III. Dealer Principal 122

25. Out with the Old 123

26. Winning Online 126

27. Top Priorities 130

28. Calling All Business Managers....................134

New Products for Old Customers: 136

29. 'On the Point' 137

30. To BDC or Not to BDC 142

31. No Traffic on the Extra Mile......................146

About the Author 150

Mosley Automotive Training Solutions 151

Contact Information 154

Introduction

What kind of sales professional, manager or dealer are you going to typify? What major goals would you like to achieve? Have you written them down? Have you even had that conversation with yourself yet?

As you might have noticed by now, optimism is back in our industry. But if you have plans to cash in on the big year the pundits are predicting, you will have to stretch yourself. As the saying goes, "To do something you've never done, you have to be someone you've never been."

I subscribe to the philosophy that it's 80 percent psychology and 20 percent mechanics — a potentially controversial view, you might say. But think about it: How effective would someone be if a trainer loaded him or her up with the best word-tracks and rebuttals in the business, but that person didn't believe or, worse yet, care about what he or she was doing?

What am I getting at? To answer, let me review how the right mindset for three critical positions will always trump mechanics:

Salesperson

To be successful this year, you must be focused on enhancing the customer experience and your own personal brand. You will also need to rethink your belief system when it comes to closing sales and asking for gross. Success also will require fine-tuning your interpretation of what a customer really wants.

As you know, I'm a big advocate of continuing education. However, I believe you can have a breakout year without learning a single new word-track or sales technique. What will make a difference is a shift in your belief system, which means breaking through myths such as, "Customers buy within 72 hours of visiting a dealership" and "You've got one shot to sell them." It also means breaking through the idea that a prospect isn't interested and shouldn't be followed up with if he or she hasn't returned your call after one or two attempts.

The problem is, those beliefs are still being employed daily, and they're costing salespeople a lot of money. What you need to do is break down what you need to sell by year, month, week and day, and map out long-term goals to achieve results.

Sales Manager

The decisions that sales managers make on a daily basis can make or break a dealership. In my opinion, too many sales managers use fear or archaic control methods to engage salespeople, which can be ineffective. "Leadership by example" needs to be the name of your game.

One of the biggest challenges for the sales staff is working with a manager who thinks his or her title means he or she has nothing left to learn. This is another psychological issue — and myth — that kills the incomes of managers and the teams they lead. As a manager, ask yourself: When is the last time I brought something new to my team to help them and myself?

Dealer Principal

Most dealers today aren't new to the game. Many of the names we know are generational and, in most cases, have been successful for a long time. However, with time comes complacency, an aversion to change and a resistance to taking risks. As the title of leadership coach Marshall Goldsmith's 2007 book reads, "What Got You Here Won't Get You There."

Now, that doesn't mean you have to abandon your principles and fundamentals. What it does mean is that you must accept that you don't have all the answers to make your dealership better and that it's okay to seek out and trust people who do.

I will leave you with this final thought: The next time you look at a plate of bacon and eggs, realize that while the chicken was involved, the pig was committed. Which one will define you?

"**Self-assessment** is a powerful tool, it allows you to be **honest with yourself FREE from outside influence** in your own space."

- CORY MOSLEY

I Sales and Selling

1. Sweat the Small Stuff

In 1997, the late Richard Carlson, Ph.D., wrote a book titled, "Don't Sweat the Small Stuff … and it's all small stuff." I know the book was one of the fastest selling titles of all time, but while the idea of not sweating the small stuff sounds good in a holistic approach, it's not so great in professional application.

In our business, the small stuff really does matter. And when that small stuff is left unchecked, it can snowball into big stuff. I know what you're thinking: "Cory, I've got talent. I've got word-tracks and rebuttals. I'm a closer." Maybe you are all of those things, but can you tie a tie properly and iron that dealership-branded polo shirt?

Unless you are a high profile person who's established such dominance in your field that your appearance doesn't matter (think Steve Jobs), it's the total package that drives the presentation. And you wouldn't want all that great training and practice you put into your pitch muted by things you thought weren't important, would you? Hey, when it comes to customer engagement, everything counts.

Real Life Is the Best Teacher

I remember it like it was yesterday. I was going to lease a new car for my wife and I walked into a highline dealership to discuss my options. I was greeted by a salesperson that, on paper, had a lot of experience selling cars, particularly the brand he represented. He looked like a mature individual who was married with children. Unfortunately, I couldn't look past the top button on his shirt being undone and the tie he had wrapped around it. It was just plain ridiculous.

So what do you think happened during his quasi-presentation of the vehicle?

Well, instead of listening to what he had to say, my focus was on his appearance. And that impacted my opinion of him, the dealership and, in a small way, the brand he was selling. Could he not notice my irritation? And how could his manager allow him to greet customers looking so disheveled?

During a recent visit to a Ferrari store, I walked through the facility to observe the amenities of the dealership. I was given a mini-bottle of Kirkland water (a Costco brand), and there were some Doritos available for me to snack on. I was shocked. Don't get me wrong, I'm not knocking Costco water and I love a bag of Doritos with a submarine sandwich like the next guy. But that wasn't the experience I expected to receive from a Ferrari dealership.

The water should match the brand and the Doritos should have been biscotti. Yes, the small things matter in the purchase experience. If a customer can buy, then the next decision he or she has to make is where to buy.

Small Things Become Big Things

There is a saying, "Success leaves clues." That's also true when we fail to accomplish our goals. Logically, the person who doesn't care about his or her appearance doesn't care about his or her presentation and customer, and the cycle just continues. At the end of the day, it becomes about mindset and the belief that one thing can be overlooked because of something else. Unfortunately, that's not how things work.

Self-Assess

Self-assessment is a powerful tool because it allows you to be honest with yourself free from outside influence and in the privacy of your own space. So walk yourself down the path you take daily and examine the pieces that make up your presentation to the world. Think about the shortcuts you took, the skipped steps. Then challenge yourself to start doing the things you should be doing but stopped.

I challenge you to raise the bar and your standards. Break from the comfort zone that has become your daily routine and push yourself into unchartered territory. Look, gains in your career and life don't come from where we have been and what we've done; they come from where we are going to go and what we are going to do.

By the way, Carlson wrote another book titled, "Easier than You Think... Because Life Doesn't have to be so Hard." In it, he lays out 39 ways in which we can take control of our day-to-day experiences. Carlson's main message is that rather than embarking on lengthy self-improvement projects, try making smaller, simpler adjustments. See, even Carlson realized that it really is the little things that matter.

2. Challenge Yourself

I doubt Janet Jackson was thinking about the car business when she wrote, "What Have You Done for Me Lately." But the title of her 1986 single sums up our industry, because everyone from the showroom salesperson to the advisor on the service drive has to face that question daily.

Unfortunately, the car business can be monotonous, causing even quality sales professionals to fall into patterns that zap them of their potential. This month, I'd like to help you fight the monotony with five ways to keep you fresh and operating at your best.

1. Break Patterns: We all have patterns that we fall into. They can range from what we say to customers during the meet-and-greet to how we respond to objections. We may even fall into a pattern when we explain features and benefits. It's as if we operate on autopilot sometimes, right? The problem is you limit your ability to adapt to situations or customer behaviors when you do.

My challenge to you is to commit to trying different approaches. So, next week, I want you to try two to three new word-tracks to explain a process, feature or benefit to a customer. To prepare, start looking for new stories and analogies on which you can base your word-track. Then conduct some "A/B testing," a cool term used by marketers to describe a method of testing different approaches on a targeted audience to see which garners a better response. Hey, the key to getting a few more deals every month could be a simple change in approach, so give it a try.

2. Be Likeable: Being likeable is like "relationship glue," but you have to stay likeable from the first interaction to the last. Being likeable means you have to be nice, respectful, enthusiastic, confident and, most importantly, authentic. The age of salespeople just being actors is either dead or dying so be yourself because everyone else is taken. You also have to be there for your customer. Just make sure you're doing it with a smile.

3. Deliver More Value: You can never deliver too much value. Many sales professionals believe that sharing information is a bad thing. Their belief is based on the idea that the more information you provide a customer, the more they'll shop you and buy elsewhere. If you share this fear, then you are probably locked into a pattern that is preventing you from being likeable, which probably means you're not creating enough value to make a prospect feel obligated to do business with you. Remember, the key to sales is to provide more value than what the prospect is expecting.

4. Understand Competitive Perceptions: In my opinion, one of the great opportunities you have to build value and close business is when a prospect brings up competitive vehicles. We could probably agree it's silly to think a prospect isn't looking at vehicles other than yours.

So, what sources are your customers using to get their information? You have to believe the salesperson at the store you're competing against is one source. The internet is another obvious source of information. But let's focus on the information coming out of the showroom, because that's where excitement is created or killed.

I remember selling the Geo Prizm (yes, I am dating myself a bit), which was basically the Toyota Corolla for about $1,300 less. I also remember watching as salespeople tried to sell the car without finding out if the customer had looked at a Corolla. If they had, they could have used that knowledge to sell them on a vehicle that touted Toyota-like reliability but for $1,000 less. I wasn't the greatest salesperson back when I was a green pea, but I was smart enough to sell a bunch of Prisms by understanding the competitive landscape and selling for and against consumer perceptions.

5. Follow Up: The mind-boggling thing about follow-up is we all know the benefits, yet many sales pros fail in the consistent execution of this critical sales-generating practice. Hey, there is something to be said about being the last man (or woman) standing. Without even working on the quality of your follow up, you can win additional business every month by simply not giving up on a customer.

See, long-term follow-up creates obligation, and obligation can sell you a bunch of additional units. The key is to focus on staying relevant. Just make sure you have something to say other than asking the customer if he or she has made a decision yet.

Everybody talks about game changers in our business, but you don't need a game changer. What you really need is incremental business that is predictable and sustainable. So challenge yourself to make it happen.

3. Showroom Confidential

When summer arrives that means "all hands on deck." But those hands need to be motivated, dedicated and, most importantly, competent. That conceit was reinforced for me after a recent car accident gave me the opportunity to experience the car-buying process as a customer.

It was my first real accident since I scratched my Toyota demo's bumper back in the '90s. Luckily, no one was injured, but I was sure I was facing a total loss with my wife's SUV this time around.

Even at this stage in my career, I consider myself a student of the business. So I didn't contact any of my dealer friends or "insiders" to get a good deal. Instead, my wife and I visited a couple of local dealership to get the full customer experience. Here are my three takeaways from my visits.

1. Adjust to the Customer's Process: I had certain things I wanted to accomplish, which meant I didn't have time for the traditional road to the sale. If you have ever met me, you know I am pretty easy to deal with. So my desire to complete my agenda shouldn't make me "difficult" in the salesperson's eyes.

Two things typically happen when a sales professional tries to shove a regimented process down the customer's throat: First, they create an adversarial situation by dismissing a decisive buyer as a "grinder" and treating them accordingly. Second, even if you make the sale, you do so at the expense of CSI, repeat business and referrals.

Make no mistake, people buy from other people for many reasons. Many times, it's not likeability. I'm certainly a process-driven individual; however, all processes require flexibility vs. a battle of wills.

2. Reduce the Time to First Pencil: At one store, it took so long to get a number that I used Twitter to inform the manufacturer about it while I was waiting. But getting numbers quickly wasn't just this dealership's problem. In fact, it seemed to be an epidemic in the area.

A couple of the stores we visited used desk tools that print out multiple payment options. I can't understand what could possibly take 10 to 20 minutes to calculate, especially when the showrooms I visited were empty.

Taking too long to present numbers creates a host of obvious problems. The buying excitement you established during the test drive begins to fade, and the customer's anxiety begins to increase. Ultimately, any delay can cost you a deal, add tension to negotiations and lower your CSI.

28

I'm not sure who teaches salespeople to drag out the numbers presentation. In my opinion, it's the wrong approach. I was so agitated by the wait at one dealership that I didn't even want to consider the deal, no matter how good it was. I view a quick and easy presentation of numbers as a sign of professionalism and respect for my time. Expediency also boosts my confidence in doing business with that operation.

Organizations that focus on efficient and timely service generally have measures in place to track speed. Think of the time counters at drive-thru windows or the salons that track time with customers down to the billable hour. Do you actually know how long it takes to work a deal in your store? Don't you agree that "time to pencil" is an important factor in selling more cars at higher gross to more satisfied customers?

3. Areas of Commendation: In most cases, several things were done right. I'm talking about things like an unrushed test drive, an introduction to a manager, offering dealership amenities and explaining service after the sale. But it only takes one cow to derail the whole train.

The reality is most customers are non-confrontational by nature. They will visit a restaurant, have a bad experience, leave a tip and never come back. They don't do "alpha" things like ask to speak to a manager, demand a free meal, and write letters, blog or tweet. They just move on. This happens in dealerships every day. We know these customers as the going-to-hold-off-on-making-a-decision type — at least that's what they say when you conduct your follow-up call. The problem is they may be holding off for 36 months, during which they'll be driving the new car they leased from your competitor.

Incidentally, as luck would have it, my wife's car wasn't totaled after all. We will be back in the market in a few years, and we'll find out how much our local dealerships have improved their processes.

4. Hunter to Influencer

How do you approach a sale? Do you hunt for customers or do you lead them down the road to a sale? The magazine's resident sales expert weighs in.

Complaints about salespeople are a common affair in the car business. If it's not the back office of the dealership, it's the customers, online reviewers and even consumer media who are taking shots at front-end staffers. But as we in the business know, nothing happens until something is sold.

The sale is the lifeblood of everything we do. F&I products, service and parts can't be sold without a sale, which means there would be no need for accounting or good customer service. And just think about your dealership's marketing efforts, which are designed to create sales and buyer awareness of your marquees and the products and services you sell.

But no matter how effective your marketing efforts are, nothing really matters unless a salesperson can convert a lead into a sale. And there are many schools of thought on how to convert a "hand raiser" into a sale. Some believe word-tracks are the key, others believe it takes great marketing, coupons and other incentives.

I have another theory.

I'd like to talk about the psychological theory of a sale. This entails establishing influence over a customer so you, as a sales professional, can deliver a better buying experience. And let me tell you, following this practice can make things a lot easier.

The Return of Authenticity

It scares me to think of some of the things we have been taught in this industry. For instance, have you ever been told that salespeople are just like actors? Hey, I loved "Rocky" just as much as the next guy, but Sly Stallone is certainly not winning any leading man award anytime soon.

The only link I can see between car people and actors — at least the ones regularly up for Oscars — is that the best actors spent years in acting school and theatre before you ever saw them at your local Cineplex. So, the question is, what school do automotive sales professionals attend to develop their skills?

Look, this is the age of authenticity, which means you need to be more genuine and more natural with customers. See, our job is to help reduce the anxiety of making such a big purchase. And if you can do that, you will drive more sales, higher gross and more satisfied customers. The point is, be yourself, because everyone else's persona is taken.

Gaining Influence

If you've been in the car business, you either have been confronted by or are a 'Type A' personality. These individuals have the natural instincts to be a closer. The problem is that people with this type of personality tend to think of themselves as hunters, and their customers as their prey. That works for a motivational rally, but that approach is poison in the showroom.

See, the difference between an influencer and a hunter is a hunter only thinks about the sale, which, in turn, creates sales resistance. I challenge you to instead present ideas in favor of the customer, and to use creativity and empathy to differentiate yourself from the competition.

One thing you'll find about the influencer's approach is that it doesn't require that you overcome objections in the traditional sense, which usually plays out like a tennis match: The customer smashes their objection to your side and you smash it back with a rebuttal.

As an 'influencer,' you are simply responding to the customer's objection with a "Here's another way to look at it" scenario. You're being empathetic to the customer's concern to make the undesirable desirable. So, the key is to connect with their values while still moving the sale forward.

Successful influence creates emotion, which allows the prospect to justify a purchase logically. So, don't be too concerned about what your customer thinks about what you say. Instead, think about how they feel about the things you say. Just remember, the head is attached to the price and the heart is attached to the wallet. Happy selling!

5. Becoming Influential

In sales, you can use any word or series of words to describe what it takes to get a commitment and close the sale. Personally, I believe it all circles back to influence. In some people's minds, the word "influence" stirs up negative thoughts, as does the word "control," but I'm not sure why.

As a manager or leader at your dealership, you must become the chief influencer if you expect your sales team to influence their customers. There are many theories about how to accomplish this. For some, fear is the great motivator; others take the 'inmates are running the asylum' approach.

There are three qualities of an influencer:

1. Motivates others to change.
2. Replaces bad behaviors with new skills.
3. Makes things happen.

How many of those qualities I listed do you possess?

How did you ascend to your leadership role at the dealership and what new skills have you learned along the way?

Most big problems succumb to changes in just a few behaviors, and the key to unlocking your team's potential can be found in a few easy-to-reach areas. Just remember what the late Steve Jobs once said: "You cannot mandate productivity, you must provide the tools to allow people to become their best."

1. Make Change Inevitable: We spend so much time in our own bubble that we miss the millions of things going on around us. Sometimes you just have to stick out your head like a periscope and see what's new. I'm always amazed when I reach out to dealers I know to get them to attend my live seminars. They always tell me they don't need another workshop on process improvement, yet I know them well enough to know that they do. My question to them is: What happens when you wake up one day and the game has completely changed?

2. Sources of Influence: The key to motivation is to identify what influences an individual. It could be the people that rely on them, or their own competitive spirit. Let's take a look at four key sources of influence:

Personal Motivation: The job is monotonous and can easily lead to burnout. It's easy to go down that path, but you must resist. You've got people counting on you, looking up to you and feeding off your energy. Speed of the leader, speed of the team, right? To avoid falling into a funk, try reading a book, attending a seminar or team-building event, or listening to a motivational audio book. The one thing I know for sure is that all the elements we need to succeed have already been written about and are readily accessible.

Personal Ability: Have you ever heard the saying, "Much of will is skill"? Many times we mistakenly attribute someone's success to being "in the zone" or just sheer determination or willpower. The reality is that success is the magnification of the skills that individual already possesses. I don't care how much willpower I have, I'm not beating Kobe Bryant in a game of H-O-R-S-E. To get more out of your time, try doing things in intervals. This will help you stay focused, while also breaking the mastery of new skills into mini goals that are attainable.

Social Motivation: Start a LinkedIn page and connect with those on a forward trajectory. Find a mentor and expand your social footprint. It's amazing how motivated you can become when you are around successful people.

Structural Motivation: Engage your team with an approach that speaks to their need to be compensated and recognized. So, bring back the salesperson of the month award, those team dinners and other events. Heck, try asking about a team member's kids once in a while. One of my go-to analogies involves the safety routine flight attendants run through before every takeoff. When they get to the part about the oxygen mask, they always instruct you to put your oxygen mask on first before helping others. There is no greater analogy for leading your team to victory. Your team shouldn't have sharper skills than you, because you should be learning and then passing those skills down — not recycling things you learned 10, 15 or 20 years ago.

Competition is fierce and the nimble, skilled, up-to-date team leaders have a huge opportunity to increase market share and then retain those customers for years to come. So get to work.

6. Execution Plan

The sales game is constantly changing. New products, marketing ideas and technology solutions continue to flow into the market, pulling dealership decision makers in several different directions: There are the short-term and long-term issues to contend with which oftentimes puts "right-now" strategies and long-range planning in conflict.

The right-now plans are often hatched in brainstorming meetings dealers hold with their management teams, ad agency or 20 Group. But coming up with a plan (or the idea of a plan) is just the first step.

What happens next is critical to the success of the idea, as how that plan is executed will ultimately determine the level of success that can be reaped from your strategy. Some pretty smart guys over at consulting firm Franklin Covey have drilled down the four key disciplines of execution and I would like to share them with you.

1. Focus on the wildly important: Ultimately, execution starts with focus. Without it, the other three will no longer matter. In the dealership environment, think about taking on a task like changing your pricing strategy or your road-to-the-sale steps. Or just think about your business development center (BDC). Change is constant in that department, right? And when change is required, we have to figure out how to make several pieces fit together before we can make changes and realize any type of ROI.

The best attack strategy is one that focuses on one or two goals that will make the most difference, rather than dividing your efforts among a dozen objectives. Now, this doesn't mean setting aside the things you must do on a daily basis to run your dealership or department. You just need to narrow the number of goals you are attempting to accomplish beyond the day-to-day demands.

2. Act on the lead measures: The easiest way to drill down on Discipline Two to is to think of it as the discipline of leverage. Lead measures are defined by the activities most connected to achieving a given goal. How many times have you called your team in to discuss the status of a new initiative but find out that one person thought the other person was handling one of the tasks?

3. Keep a compelling scoreboard: This discipline is about keeping your team engaged in the goal at hand. And the way to do that is to make sure everyone knows the score at all times. Everyone involved in the effort should be able to tell whether or not they are winning. Most dealerships have a sales board listing the month's objectives and the latest individual stats. The same holds true across all dealership departments and initiatives. Great teams know their status at any given moment. If they don't, they can't know what they need to do to win the game.

4. Create a cadence of accountability: The final discipline requires the establishment of a frequently recurring cycle that accounts for past performance and planning to move the score forward. Only at this stage can execution actually happen. Disciplines One, Two and Three set up the game, but your team won't be in the game until you apply accountability.

But there's more to execution than simply displaying an ability to set a goal and achieve it. You must also account for the raging whirlwind of daily life. To go one step further, the odds of successfully executing a strategy decrease when more people become involved. Got any "old-school" thinkers at your dealership? Yeah, they can make it harder to succeed, too. Ultimately, true accountability means making personal commitments to your entire team: first to move the scores forward, then to follow through in a disciplined way.

My mother use to love the term "buckle down" when she'd kindly encouraged me to get focused or get it together. It's safe to say that no matter which department we represent in the dealership, we sometimes need to buckle down and take a more systematic approach to getting things done.

"It's not what they

THINK

it's how they

FEEL

that will

INCREASE

your

PROFITS"

— CORY MOSLEY

7. The 'New' Road to a Sale

If you don't have your showroom act down, shame on you.
If you need a little help with handling Internet and phone-in
leads, then read on.

When it comes to handling Internet leads, the rules of
engagement are still evolving. But the core rules of the sales
game remain the same. I'm frequently asked what the best
strategy for selling online is, or what my personal "best
practices" are. My response is that I stick to a three-part
process: e-mail, phone, and showroom.

Sounds simple, right? Well, that's because it is. From my
observations while working in different stores around the
country, I've noticed that we sometimes search for the
magic bullet instead of utilizing the remedy that's sitting
right in front of us. We buy expensive treatments for a
wound and forget that the aloe tree growing on the kitchen
window sill works just as well.

I've seen determined sales professionals and business
development center reps work deals by phone, or send
extremely long e-mails, only to be discouraged when a
customer doesn't respond or buys a car from a competitor.

Naturally, the salesperson or rep thinks the fault lies with the customer, but the real culprit is the salesperson. And without a sound strategy for driving business over the Internet, they'll continue to lose sales. Let's take a closer look at a few key ways to approach this.

You've Got Mail: One of the keys to e-mail is to create engagement. The goal should not be to sell the car. Rather, it should be viewed as an opportunity to start separating yourself from the competition. This is where you'll set the expectations and lay the groundwork for the next steps. Good e-mail etiquette and the ability to move a customer to the next step comes from understanding two main principles of sales communication: Effective communication explains, and persuasive communication sells.

For instance, consider all those enticing credit card offers many of us receive in the mail. I'm sure you're familiar with the ones offering low APR rates or quadruple points for spending a certain amount. Those offers are written by creative writers because they are designed to persuade you.

Now, once you sign up, you'll get a letter in the mail with your new card. The letter inside unfolds like an accordion to reveal pages of small print detailing the terms and conditions. These words are written by technical writers and explain what will and won't happen with the card. Now, which writer are you when you send out those e-mails? Are you persuading or communicating? This is a critical determination, so give it some thought and ask for someone else's opinion.

On the Horn: Interacting with a customer over the phone represents an opportunity for you to establish value and gain control of the process. "Control" is not a bad word. In fact, lack of control contributes to the loss of gross and blown deals on a daily basis.

Winning the phone game is all about conversion. You must compel the customer to take the next step. To create greater influence, you need to make a greater impact when discussing what's in it for the customer if they make an appointment to visit the store.

You also should eliminate "wish" questions from your vocabulary. "Have you driven yet?" and "Are you familiar with the options?" are classic examples. Asking these questions means you're wishing for a "No" answer. And if you get that response, that's your cue to utter that line I detest the most: "Come on down."

So, what do you do when the customer says yes to those questions? You know where that conversation is headed: Death Valley, otherwise known as "What's your best price?" land.

Consider using strategies that revolve around the value in visiting the showroom or the promise of a different or better experience. Schedule them for a VIP appointment or tell them about the things you will do for them prior to their arrival that will make their no-obligation shopping experience better.

Get Them to the Showroom: I'm going to assume that you know what to do once a customer visits your showroom, which is why I focused more on converting e-mail and phone-in leads. Consider focusing more on the customer experience than the road to the sale and you will reap the benefits of these new opportunities. It may sound touchy-feely, but a wise man once taught me that it's not about what you or I like, it's simply about what the customer responds to the best. Find it, and do more of it!

8. Self-Sabotaging Behaviors to Avoid

Working in the car business is a unique experience. Outsiders just don't understand the daily pressures we face, right? The reality is, for all the things that make our business special, selling a car is no different than selling copy machines or a bottle of Snapple. You're just meeting with customers and helping them buy something they want, right? OK, not even I believe that. Not all of it, anyway.

See, the underlying goal might be the same, but there are several other duties that add to the complexity of selling cars. We must manage the customer while making sure they're satisfied enough with the experience that they'll return for their next vehicle. There also are closing techniques to perfect and paperwork to complete. How good you are at completing those tasks often will separate you from the rest.

With that in mind, let's take a look at some other key areas that divide the best from the rest. I call them the "7 Self-Sabotaging Behaviors to Avoid." If you've successfully avoided them, you're probably one of the superstars at your dealership. Here are the first five:

1. Failing to Adequately Prepare: I too came from the showroom, and I know there is time in the typical sales floor schedule to adequately prep yourself to serve your customers. Just remember that preparedness comes in many shapes and sizes, from product knowledge and knowing the ideal buyer for each model to memorizing the latest incentives, rebates and vehicle accolades.

Unfortunately, most salespeople feel like they can learn as they go. These are people who hate taking tests, being called on to answer questions or participating in role-playing exercises. The excuse I often hear from these individuals is, "I don't do well with role playing. I need a live customer to show my stuff." Listen, your skill needs to be instant and ready for an audience of one or one thousand. As the old saying goes, "Practice makes perfect."

2. Being Phony: I know many of you have heard that salespeople are a lot like actors, but, frankly, I can't imagine how someone could like, respect and trust you without some level of authenticity. To make the deal happen, you have to be who you are, not just what you think the customer wants you to be.

3. Misidentifying the Stage in the Prospect's Decision-Making Process: I see this all the time. A commitment from the customer has yet to be established and the salesperson is already discounting the car by $2,000 and throwing in free oil changes. Remember, most customer decisions boil down to two things: deciding whether to change (buying a new car), and then deciding with whom to make that change (which dealership to buy from).

The question you need to answer is: Do you offer something the customer wants? If you don't, then you still have a lot of work to do. Price will never prevail in a scenario when the first stage has not been properly handled.

4. Forcing the Close: Naturally, closing the sale is the name of the game. But pushing too hard can ruin your chances of success. Sometimes, just moving on to the next step in the process can get the customer to make a decision. So, instead of hitting them between the eyes with an "Are you buying today?" why not just start doing some paperwork? You'd be amazed at how many times customers will start to close themselves.

5. Neglecting the Long-Term Client: The true sales professional is always looking to expand his or her client base, especially in the "What have you done for me lately" environment in which we work. Unfortunately, that approach tends to narrow our focus on what is in front of us, so we forget about the long-term benefits of sending letters for birthdays and vehicle anniversaries, or reaching out to a sold customer who just had his or her vehicle serviced at the dealership.

I received a text the other day from a salesperson who told me about a $4,000 gross he secured on a Saturday deal. How'd he do it? He started chatting with a customer in the service drive, and made a strong case for the customer trading in his 2008 model for a 2011. This is an everyday story, but is it an everyday story for you?

6. Personal Accountability: Yes, I've written about these two dirty little words in past columns, but that's because they're very important to what we do. And whenever I train sales managers on the differences between really leading and merely managing, I always ask the question: "When is the last time any salesperson came up to you and said, 'Boss, I messed this deal up?'" The room invariably erupts in laughter because it almost never happens — but it really should.

Whether or not you like to play the blame game when it comes to deals gone badly, it's important, as a manager, that you identify what went wrong. A salesperson may not want to admit that his or her actions, approach, techniques, word-tracks or even body language played a role in sabotaging a deal.

The point I'm trying to make here is that you shouldn't think about deals gone bad as lost opportunities. Instead, look at them — and this may sound touchy-feely — as an opportunity to teach and learn. See, you want to separate yourself from other sales professionals and grow. The way to do that is to examine what went right and what went wrong in the deal; the problem is most of us do not take the time to evaluate. We would rather just be done and look ahead to the next deal.

7. Know-It-All Syndrome: There's nothing that drives me crazier than a salesperson or manager who thinks he or she knows it all. Let me be clear: Being in the business for 20 or 30 years means absolutely nothing in today's marketplace, especially if you're not adapting, changing, expanding and implementing new skills. Don't let your past success fool you!

One of my go-to quotes when speaking to dealers is one I picked up from Bill Gates. The first big step he made toward building his billion-dollar empire was to license the DOS operating system — which he didn't even own — to IBM, under a deal that would allow him to license it to other companies as well.

See, the smart people at IBM believed the real money was in computer hardware, not software. Well, you know how that worked out. Gates summed up the lesson learned thusly: "Success is a menace. It convinces smart people they can't lose."

If you are good at what you do, congratulations! However, don't think in terms of effective vs. ineffective; instead, focus on ways to become more effective. Put yourself in a continuous learning mode. Hey, I've got 11 books in queue on my desk right now, waiting to be read. How about you?

Know-it-all syndrome is mainly caused by sales professionals and managers who don't think beyond the fundamentals. I'm not here to challenge the road to the sale or the fundamental principles that have made millions of sales pros, including myself, successful in the car business. But in this day and age, walking around with the belief that the demands, needs, wants and interests of customers haven't changed is simply crazy.

Listen, the competition for customers in today's marketplace is fierce. Don't just run with the pack, lead it! I think you deserve it.

9. The Four 'Cs' of Phone Prospecting

Whenever the topic of phone skills and sales professionals comes up, the conversation seems to end with the same conclusion: Showroom sales professionals simply aren't good at working the phones. In their defense, I will say that it's not their fault. The real problem is simply a deficiency of knowledge.

If you know better and choose not to do better, shame on you. Just because you understand the "road to the sale" doesn't automatically mean you can handle a phone "up." First off, most salespeople are trained to sell face to face. The difference between doing that and selling over the phone is the level of control a customer feels when he or she is not talking to you face to face.

I'm sure you've heard the term "peel them off of the ceiling." If you haven't, it basically describes a technique where the salesperson kicks off a sale by presenting really high numbers. This gives the salesperson a psychological advantage that will keep the customer in the showroom. And to make sure the customer's kids don't distract, there are sales managers available to provide entertainment or a game room to keep the kids busy.

The problem with using this technique with a phone "up" is you don't have those factors available to keep the customer on the phone. What ends up happening is the salesperson gives his or her best rendition of that old sales line, "Come on down and don't forget to ask for me."

To help with your phone skills, let's take a look at four core fundamentals — each of which just happens to start with the letter "C" — that will make you more successful with phone prospects.

1. Confidence

This is obviously a no-brainer. However, you would be surprised at how many unsure salespeople pick up the phones every day and fumble through calls about inventory, rebates and incentives, then hammer their message home with a "Would you like to come on down?" Lack of confidence leaves the door open for a customer to assert control, which, of course, is a big no-no. The easiest way to head that off is to actually fill in the missing information that caused you to lose confidence in the first place. If you are stumbling through information about lease options, then it would only make good sense to spend a few minutes a day going over the latest lease programs.

2. Credibility

We already face an uphill battle based on the simple fact that we are in the car business. It's not who we are but what we do that people hold against us. An innocent mistake can spell doom when working with a prospect on the phone or in the showroom. Just like confidence, the easiest way to be credible is to invest the time to actually know what you are talking about.

3. Competence

By now, you probably realize that all of these factors connect. Being confident feeds the appearance of being credible, and credibility will make you more competent. Competence itself boils down to the ability to handle the situation presented to you in a professional manner and to the satisfaction of the customer.

4. Congruence

The bottom line is, what you say needs to make sense to the prospect. The conversation should weave itself together and flow. Easier said than done, right? The worst thing you can do — and I know it's hard not to — is to get caught up in the script. This becomes problematic when the customer says or asks something that's not on the script, but you continue down that path anyway. When that happens, the customer will typically come back with, "What you're saying doesn't make sense." That statement usually means game over.

The name of the game when it comes to phone sales is leading. Lead the customer down the path that satisfies his or her initial reason for calling, and position them for that important next step: a visit to the showroom. Remember, you're not a customer hotline. Treat each call as an opportunity to generate sales. Breaking away from the question-and-answer mentality may indeed be the biggest challenge you will face, but shifting away from playing phone tennis with your customer to actually closing something will lead to more appointments.

"**Increasing sales** is about **incremental** and **sustainable** growth. **NOT** quick wins."

- CORY MOSLEY

10. Six Sales-Driving Ideas

If you've been reading my book you know I stress taking responsibility, setting goals and the benefits of continuing to be a good student. I want to drive that message home with what I believe are the six keys to achieving your goals:

1. Reinvent Yourself: Whether you realize it or not, you're a brand, and that brand is reflected in how you sell or manage. In fact, at this very moment, you are known for something. It could be that you're great with customers. Maybe you're a strong closer.

Now, whatever you are today doesn't have to be what you are tomorrow. Way too often, people will hide behind the idea that they are simply just the way they are, which is really an excuse to ignore their opportunity to be better. Why not try to become a specialist in trucks, SUVs or coupes and learn all there is to know about the category, including competing brands? Not only will this newfound confidence contribute to higher gross profit, it will eliminate the fear of losing deals to products of lesser quality.

2. Create Separation: When all things are equal, you have a 50/50 chance to win or lose with each prospect. While those odds may be OK on the roulette table, I doubt they will work in the showroom. That's why you need to focus on enhancing the customer experience to the maximum level. For instance, instead of telling people to "come on down," invite customers to schedule a "price and vehicle consultation, where we use all of our resources at the dealership to help you make the best car-buying decision." Doesn't that sound more intriguing?

To improve you must focus on enhancing the experience and your approach on the road to the sale. During a recent celebration for my grandparents' 60th wedding anniversary, my grandfather gave a short speech and offered a few words of wisdom about marriage that I think are extremely relevant in the sales environment. He said that the way you stay married for 60 years is to always make your wife think she's in control. The same goes for your customers, make them feel like they're in control. All it takes is a little finesse.

3. Focus on Service: It saddens me to see salespeople who spend their day staring at the door, waiting for the next "up" to come in. I don't care what you sell; every brand and dealership retains a certain percentage of its customers. It is your responsibility as a salesperson to maintain a relationship with your customers after the sale. And we all know the rewards associated with customer retention: referral business, sales to others in the household and less negotiating the second and third time around. In most cases, the result is a higher gross profit.

4. Strive for Excellence: If you don't care, who will? Strive to be the best and don't settle for anything less. And if your gauge for excellence is what others are doing, stop.

There's a story I like to tell about a salesman I once knew named Al Bowers. He could literally take half of the month off and roll 20 cars in the last week. Al, who had two phones at his desk, didn't mess around. Some salespeople were jealous of his talents, others just wanted to beat him on the monthly leader board, but never thought it was possible — well, until someone finally did.

5. Evaluate Outcomes: Start taking a look at the deals you don't make. Sales guru Zig Ziglar states that every sale has five basic obstacles to overcome: no money, no hurry, no time, no desire and no trust. Instead of simply deactivating that lost deal from your CRM system and moving on to the next customer, take a moment to reflect on which obstacle you might have failed to overcome.

6. Work the Pay plan: Do you really understand how your pay plan works? More importantly, do you know how to maximize it? If not, you could be leaving big money on the table. Are there special "spiff" cars that pay double the commission? Do you get a piece of the back-end action, but haven't taken the time to work closer with your F&I manager? Are there bonuses on aging inventory? You need to know all of these things before you work your next customer.

Finally, let's have some fun! Experts who track the business say it should be a good year for the business, so let's rock 'n' roll and make it the best year ever!

11. It's in the Presentation

Life inside the dealership is an experience only those who have been there can appreciate. Whether you are in sales or service, each department carries its own unique challenges. Let's face it, the job is monotonous. And, after every successful month, you get the pleasure of starting from zero once again. So, what can you do to be successful?

Most would agree that the answer lies in your people skills, technique and ability to adopt a mindset that stops you from falling into a "move 'em in, move 'em out" mentality. In our heart of hearts, we know the greatest rewards come as a result of staying fresh, nimble and creative. But there is one item I'd like to add to that list: presentation.

Whether you're online, on the phone or interacting with a customer face-to-face, presentation is the key to convincing them to take that next step. Let's look at some ways you can improve your presentation in those three areas:

1. Online: The name of the game here is getting the customer to take action. We in the business tend to refer to that as "conversion." The goal, of course, is to get them to submit a lead, call the store or walk into the showroom. To increase your chances of a conversion, make sure you have multiple touch points on your Website that promote engagement.

Four low-cost, high-return features you can add to your Website are a chat feature, interactive credit applications, and video and appraisal tools. You must also consider optimizing your site for Web-enabled mobile devices as their popularity continues to increase.

2. On the Phone: According to a survey conducted by Richmond, Va.-based Communication Briefings, 82 percent of respondents said their opinion about a company is influenced "a lot" by how a representative answers the phone.

This should serve notice not only to the receptionist at your dealership, but also to those sales and service professionals who take customer calls. Just remember the four "Cs" to a strong over-the-phone presentation: confidence, competence, credibility and congruence.

3. In the Showroom: The ultimate opportunity to get a deal done is when the customer is in your house (i.e., the showroom). Obviously, I don't need to rewrite the road to the sale; however, I would like to share two things I would love to see return on a massive scale to the car business:

- **The Vehicle Walk-Around:** When was the last time you gave a customer a thorough walk-around? In my last search to replace my personal vehicle, I visited five dealerships franchised by five different OEMs. Only one gave me a walk-around. No coincidence, the individual who gave me the walk-around turned out to be the No. 1 salesperson at that dealership. In fact, he outsold the next best salesperson by five cars every month.

- **Listening to Gain a Tactical Advantage:** Have you ever heard about the "psychology of sales"? It refers to our ability to influence the outcome we desire by winning the sale. As Ben Affleck's character in the movie "Boiler Room" said, "A sale is made on every call you make. Either you sell the client some stock or he sells you a reason he can't."

My point here is simple: There is useful information to be gained that will assist you in your efforts to get the customer to take action. You won't find it on the guest sheet or through the so-called "qualifying interview." Process is important, but don't sacrifice or suppress your natural abilities of observation in the name of procedure.

Regardless of what dealership you work for, most every manufacturer makes a pretty good product. Which one is best can be based on facts or simple perception. My question to you is, how sad is it to never have the opportunity to present a great product because we can't get a customer to take the next step online, in the showroom or on the phone?

Let me leave you with this: Lots of people like steak, right? But let's say I offer you a steak, season and grill it to perfection. However, instead of serving it to you on a plate, I take the lid off my garbage can, flip it over and plop your steak on it? Doesn't sound so appetizing anymore, does it? Presentation counts, so make sure you aren't serving up your great products on a trash-can lid.

12. A Basic Problem

It is a manager's favorite line: "We need to just get back to basics." While there is certainly something to be said about the benefits of mastering the basics, it is definitely not where we should be making our living in today's economy.

I used to hear with great frequency statements like, "Just get 'em in and we'll close 'em," or "We just need more traffic." Well, most of us have probably learned by now that it's not just about trying to get more traffic, it's about shifting our focus to maximizing every opportunity.

One of the definitions for the word "basic" is "offering or consisting in the minimum required." Is that really good enough in today's aggressive marketplace? Just so we're on the same page here, when I say aggressive marketplace, I'm not merely referring to the tough economy. I'm referring to the multitude of purchase options consumers have nowadays.

Think about it: How many makes and models can a consumer spend $15,000, $20,000, $50,000, $60,000, or even $70,000 on? So, if we all can agree that every "up" really does count how can we move past the basics and employ strategies to increase our sales and incomes? Well, here are my five ways to do just that:

1. Focus on Authenticity: I always applaud sales professionals who have found ways to create their own brands within their stores. I think about the sales guy in Texas who goes by "Coach," the guy in Jersey who rhymes his name "Meador" with the word "better." See, I appreciate those salespeople who are unconventional and can sell cars and make a good living because of it. Why? Because they're authentic, and authentic people focus on building long-term relationships with customers. They also are likeable and sincere, and get unsolicited referrals on a regular basis.

2. Take Responsibility for Your Own Education: It is amazing to me how many times I hear someone say they can't attend a workshop or seminar because the dealer won't pay for it. It doesn't matter how long you've been in the business, the game changes on a regular basis. That means you can't stop learning if you plan to increase your earnings. Take today's Gen-Y buyers. How much do you really know about this buying segment and the radical differences between their buying habits and motivations vs. the baby boomer generation? My guess is not much. Do you think it might be worth a $30 book or a $300 seminar to know who your future customer will be?

3. Employ the "ME + 3 Rule": This rule is one of my favorite principles to teach because it's a real eye opener for salespeople. The rule states that when communicating with a prospect; realize that there are three other dealers vying for your customer's business. So, when you leave your next voicemail or take your next sales call; remember that there are three other sales professionals who are talking to your customer. That means what you say and how you say it really matters.

4. Focus on Buying Motives: Sales trainer Zig Ziglar talks about the five selling challenges: no need, no money, no hurry, no desire and no trust. At the base of any customer objection is a failure to overcome or address one of those five challenges to the customer's satisfaction. If you focus on identifying and then speaking to a customer's motive for making the purchase, then you should be able to dramatically reduce buyer hesitation and increase your close ratios. When you're able to identify the motive and satisfy the challenges, you can elicit positive emotion from the customer. Remember, practicality causes a person to delay; emotion causes a person to take action.

5. Set and Define Your Goals: Most of us don't get in a car and start driving with no destination in mind. Why not take a step back from the daily tasks of selling to determine and write down the outcome you are seeking beyond just selling cars and making money. What are your goals? What are you about? What do you hope to achieve? What value do you want to bring to your customers? Define your service to others, what you want to accomplish, how you will get it done, and state the outcome as though it has already taken place.

We are in the business of selling cars and that requires change. A military general once said, "Those who hate change will hate irrelevance a lot more." I think that says it all.

"Those who stop

LEARNING
themselves should
BE DISQUALIFIED FROM
TEACHING"

— CORY MOSLEY

II. Sales Management

13. Signing Rookies

Locating and hiring top talent isn't as easy as it used to be. In the   past, all we needed to do was offer a great pay plan and a guaranteed salary of $200 per week, as well as a promise for greater riches in just a few short years. And all they had to do was work full days two to three times per week, every Saturday and most holidays. How can anyone turn that down, right?

Unfortunately, times have changed. You are going to have to abandon the old rules and start fresh if you want to attract new talent. That's especially true if you're looking to recruit Gen Y talent to your dealership. So, here's a quick primer on how these individuals think and what they expect from their employers.

1. They Want to Direct Themselves: Gen Y wants the opportunity to show they can get the job done without being micro-managed. Start with proper training and then allow them to get into their own groove.

2. They Demand Freedom of Schedule: This does not mean they need to be able to make their own schedule, but it does mean the traditional approach won't be sustainable.

And wouldn't it be a shame to lose talent because they couldn't get a free Saturday or two?

3. They Seek Unconventional Employment Benefits: Look for other ways to entice this group besides paying them on commission.

4. They Prioritize Lifestyle over Salary: Aside from student loans, this group hasn't had to take on all the debt and life responsibilities that drive the hunger of most salespeople. In fact, Gen Y would gladly give up a $250 spiff on a Saturday to have the day off.

5. They Want to Know They're Making a Difference: They want to know they are contributing and that you value their efforts.

6. They Want Feedback: Gen Yers want to know what's going on. But they don't want to simply be told they're doing a great job, they want to know how they can improve.

7. They Want Flexibility: "My way or the highway" won't work with this group. Rethink that strategy and learn how to be more flexible without compromising your process.

Now that we've covered what they want, let's look at the **eight things you have to do to prepare for Gen Y's arrival.**

1. Streamline Bureaucracy: Make decisions, offer direction, act on those decisions, and follow through on promises.

2. Improve Communication: Create an open-door policy and encourage two-way conversations.

3. Create a Path for Growth: It's not easy to have a promotion path unless you operate multiple locations. Even then, you are dealing with limited upward mobility. One idea is to create different levels of sales professionals based on certification, training, units sold and tenure. Start your next new hire as a "junior" salesperson and give him or her a path toward a senior-level salesperson position. You can even offer salary increases or commissions and bonuses to go along with the tiers. Whatever structure you create, creating a path for growth is how you keep talent striving for the next level.

4. Start with a Clean Slate: It's never a fun exercise, but in order to attract and retain talent, you need to put everything on the table. That includes everything from pay and work schedules to time-off and end-of-month policies. Look, this new generation thinks differently, which means we have to do the same.

5. Invest in Them Early: You can't operate with a fear of losing your people. You have to train and invest in their development. Besides, you don't want untrained people dealing with your customers. Even if you do train them and they leave, at least you got 100 percent effort from them while they were with your organization.

6. Flatter Them: In today's society, everyone gets a trophy. That means you have to encourage and compliment your Gen Y talent if you want them to give you 100 percent effort and stay with your organization.

7. Break Goals Down Into Small Wins: Don't wait until the month ends to review successes and failures with your sales teams. Assign daily and weekly tasks and check on their progress regularly throughout the month.

8. Encourage a Team Atmosphere: This provides a built-in support system that will help you retain and grow your team.

Those are the keys to attracting talented Gen Yers. And who knows? Implementing some of the policies I described might also help you retain the talented vets who just need a little encouragement.

14. The Gross Killer

The age-old battle of sales vs. service conjures up fond memories of cars stuck in service, pre-delivery inspections (PDI) left undone, missing keys, and packing all those last-minute spot deliveries on the short-staffed Saturday crew. The stories can just go on and on, but what about the gross killer that's right smack in front of us? I'm referring to the sometimes tense and abrasive relationship between sales and F&I.

Over the years, the relationship between F&I and sales has become increasingly strained. Multiplying regulations have changed the way deals get sent to the "box," and the back-end grosses just aren't what they used to be. I have to admit, I miss the days of simply writing payments in the 300s on a worksheet, getting a commitment and throwing that customer into the box so my F&I manager could work his magic.

So, what's the beef? In working with dealers around the country, I have found that the general tension between the two departments can usually be attributed to one of two scenarios:

1. From the F&I manager: "The sales department gives away my rates and works deals to the bone, so there isn't any meat left."

2. From the salesperson: "The F&I manager is moving front-end gross to the back-end so he can make money."

Any other issues are mostly superficial, such as, "The F&I manager takes too long" or "Salespeople don't schedule deliveries properly."

So, let's focus on what I believe to be the two "biggies." In most instances, I find that many salespeople don't completely understand the role F&I plays in a dealership. That's especially true when their pay plans don't involve back-end gross percentage commissions. Some of the best dealerships in the country involve the F&I manager in the structuring of a deal prior to presenting a formal offer to a prospect. The mantra amongst all sales staff should be to go for maximum profitability. Unfortunately, that thinking gets thrown right out of the window in a salesperson's self-induced desperation to get the deal done.

If your store utilizes multiple payment scenarios, does your numbers presentation automatically include payments with an extended warranty or other applicable after-sale items? If so, that type of pencil strategy maximizes total gross profit and has sales and F&I working together. If not, and you're only including a point or two rate markup, then you're ending up with a single payment with a down-to-the-penny quote, and a friendly note from the sales team that reads, "See if you can do anything with this."

It's perfectly natural for a salesperson to be concerned with the "me" factor, but it's the "we" result that keeps the lights on, the advertising flowing, and everyone's year-to-date income growing. The attitude shift is, let's care about everyone earning a living, including the F&I manager.

When it comes to the relationship between F&I and sales, reason doesn't matter. A F&I manager could never hope to have a great relationship with any salesperson if he or she knows that his or her front-end gross is now split with or moved in its entirety to the back end. Any experienced dealership manager understands that circumstances like bank approval caps and loan-to-value ratios can affect how much front-end profit is allowed and sometimes spur restructured grosses.

Unfortunately, no salesperson wants to hear any of that. This is what fuels conflict within the dealership and quickly takes sales professionals' and managers' eyes off the ball.

So what's the answer? Communication; Now may be the perfect time for managers from all departments to realign their strategies to revolve around maximizing gross profit across the board. Make your salespeople aware of all the detail that goes into the F&I process. You might even consider cross-training your sales and F&I managers. That can help to improve strategies for deal structuring so that both departments win.

Stay focused on the sum total and don't get emotional about individual deals. It's just getting too expensive to do it any other way. Success requires partnership!

15. 4.5 Success Drivers

If you were one of the more than 21,000 attendees at the National Automobile Dealers Association's annual convention, then you hopefully partied, learned and were exposed to the latest and greatest that our industry has to offer — not necessarily in that order.

Attending the event is definitely a juggling act. I personally had to keep an eye on speaking duties, meetings to expand my business and running my annual "Dealers, don't buy anything without calling me first" program. Yes, I encourage my clients to keep their American Express cards in their pockets until they touch base with me to figure out how the new tool or service they want fits into their current dealership strategy.

So, to help you do the same, I thought I'd offer you 4.5 areas that you need to strengthen this year.

I. CRM: Having been involved with CRM since 1999, it is scary to think about a dealer operating without one. The trap many dealers fall into is treating CRM like a check-off item on a to-do list. The key to CRM mastery is to be highly proficient in three key areas:

1. Daily usage of the system for both accountability and reporting
2. Executing a customer life-cycle marketing plan
3. Utilizing the data to identify training, additional business development trends and growth opportunities

The sophistication level of CRMs has certainly grown way beyond logging "ups" and sending letters. My challenge to you is to engage the management team and assess how much of your CRM you are using, and using effectively. Also consider what additional enhancements may be available to close the gaps in your sales process.

II. Human Capital: Developing your human capital through training and skill development is something most dealers know they must do, but they tend to struggle in two common areas:

1. Training being delivered is outdated, recycled and not customer-centric: You may like touting your store's daily training regimen, but what exactly are you training on? See, there are basically two forms of dealership training: process and sales. Training on how to fill out a buyers order is process training, while training on how to get a commitment so you can start filling out the form is sales training.

I always cringe when I learn that a dealership's managers are training employees on things they learned as a newbie. Think about it: If you have been a manager for 12 years and a salesperson for six years before that, then you could be passing along information that is 18 years old. The thought of those old word-tracks being passed on to the newer generation is just too scary to think about.

2. No Consistency to Training and Development: I will never forget the dealer who told me I was the first person in 12 years to conduct training at his store. I guess that's why the store kept the lights out in one section of the showroom to save money on the electric bill. When people aren't properly trained and motivated, sales suffer, gross suffers and everybody loses.

3. Efficiency: Utilizing a single-source program that can manage several aspects of your operation and eliminate unnecessary steps in any process will decrease transaction time while increasing transaction volume. Remember, the utopia of business success is to achieve more sales revenue with less labor and workload.

4. Digital: It's mind-boggling how fast the digital game changes. Heck, I'll bet the game will have changed by the time you read this column. My suggestion to you is to vet your potential providers hard and find a trusted source of information. Also, the rules about jacks-of-all trades haven't changed, so be open to vendor partners who specialize in certain aspects of digital.

4.5. Culture: New momentum and energy can help you assess the work environment. Try a survey using SurveyMonkey, and look for trends and opportunities to create a better work environment.

Now, don't be cynical and think all the feedback is going to revolve around employees who just want you to pay them more money. There could be some real issues you are unaware of. And hey, if your employees are satisfied, you can bet your current and potential customers will also be satisfied for years to come.

"If you want **BETTER RESULTS**
from your **FOLLOW-UP**
JUST REMEMBER THAT

VISIBLE EQUALS
VALUABLE"

— CORY MOSLEY

16. Dead or Alive?

The year was 2006. I was working with dealers to develop and promote e-mail marketing campaigns. At the time, our industry was doing a horrible job of collecting and leveraging customer e-mails to drive sales and service-lane business. Today, the same companies I used to work with on those campaigns are now listed as part of the portfolios of the big powerhouse companies in our industry.

And let's face it, automotive retail has never been known as living on the cutting edge. We tend to wait until something's been proven before incorporating it into our operations. That led me to ask this question: In today's social media-driven world, where does e-mail fit into a dealer's marketing strategies? I posed that question and more to two industry experts, my friends Paul Potratz of Potratz Partners Advertising and Peter Martin with Cactus Sky Communications. Here's what they had to say:

Mosley: A few years ago, e-mail marketing was the "it" thing. What is it today?

Martin: E-mail has changed dramatically. For one, it is much harder to get an e-mail delivered into an inbox. If it is a

Gmail or Yahoo! address, it is almost impossible unless you do everything right. Unfortunately, 20 percent of the e-mails in most dealers' lead and prospect databases are Gmail and Yahoo! accounts.

And if you're trying to e-mail your customers using a CRM system, a majority of your prospects aren't going to receive your e-mails. You also run the risk of getting blacklisted if you continue using your CRM system to send out e-mail promotions. See, Internet service providers are looking at the quality of the list. And what we are finding is that 30 percent of our clients' e-mail lists are invalid, which is a huge problem if you're using that list to market.

Potratz: It's a shiny nickel. What I mean by that is, yes, e-mail marketing makes more sense today than it did a year ago. And that's due to the explosion of Smartphone's and tablets. Now you can even track a customer's digital body language and automate e-mail promotions based on his or her behavior, which should make your lead conversion better than ever before.

Mosley: Then what is the best way to utilize e-mail marketing?

Martin: E-mail is still the most cost-effective way to reach customers, but it needs to be done properly. People who are just sending out mass e-mails and not following the rules are going to encounter lower response rates and problems.

Mosley: How does social media factor into the effectiveness of a dealer's e-mail marketing efforts?

Martin: From what we've seen, it has had no impact. However, e-mail can be used very effectively to build social communities.

Mosley: Do you see social media marketing eventually overtaking or phasing out e-mail marketing?

Martin: No. Social media is great for generating exposure, but using e-mail for marketing is still your best solution for delivering an interactive marketing message to customers.

I recently attended a conference where a top person from Twitter made a controversial comment about "buying" followers. He said it was good because only a small portion of your followers will ever see something that you post. And that's why e-mail marketing is still a viable option, because while your Twitter followers may have interest in your dealership, an e-mail campaign reaches your customers and prospects that have shown an interest in your products.

Potratz: Social media has not replaced e-mail marketing; rather, they simply complement each other. Social media marketing offers targeted opportunities. Combine that with e-mail and you will become top of mind for the majority of customers in your CRM. There's also Facebook remarketing, which can increase awareness of your brand and lead conversions. Just remember, it is not the quantity of your messages but the quality.

Mosley: Should dealers be focused on being first or perfecting each strategy one by one?

Potratz: Google changes their algorithm every 17.5 hours, so being first would be a little difficult. However, if you have a keen understanding of shopper behavior, being the first will add to your strategy.

Now, I used the word "strategy," but, in my experiences, only one out of 125 dealers actually has a strategy in place. It can be a daunting task, but it is a necessary task. Otherwise, you will get pulled into the shiny-nickel buying process.

17. Three Traffic Drivers

With demand on the upswing, it's time to decide whether to wait for customers to find you or to read our sales insider's recommendations for reeling them in.

Not a bad first quarter, right? Optimism was high and all signs point to better times ahead. So, what does this mean to you and your dealership? Well, it would be easy to adopt a laissez-faire approach and let traffic and 'brand interest' determine your sales fate. But we all know that's not an option.

Still, after all your hard work through the lean years, I wouldn't blame you for relying on attractive incentives, robust manufacturer advertising and good luck. But just in case you are the proactive type, I thought I'd list out three key business drivers that can help improve your odds as the key summer selling season approaches.

1. Database Marketing Strategy: Yeah, you've heard it before, you've probably tried it, and you may have had some success. Well, I'm here to tell you that there is a big difference between knowing something and actually executing on it.

See, in order to mine that gold stored on your DMS, you need a strategy and process that goes beyond the basics. So, to get you on the right path, here are three questions to consider and answer before you draw up those plans:

Question 1: What type of database marketing are you doing now? Your strategy should cover letters, phone calls and e-mails based on the customer information you can pull from your database. This will allow you to take immediate action once you've identified a prospect.

Question 2: Are you using finance data to target buyers? A great way to create a better prospect is to use better information. So, instead of sending out generic trade-in, trade-up, trade-out letters, use your data to determine which customers are in a positive equity position. This will not only allow you to improve the value proposition you're offering, it will create a stronger call to action for the customer.

Question 3: What's your strategy for marketing to your lease portfolio? Many dealerships look at their lease maturity list on a rolling, 30-day basis. Unfortunately, that leaves them vulnerable to customers trading out their vehicle before they can be reached. Getting an early start isn't always the right answer either.

The problem I see with most 30-day plans is they start and end with asking the customer what they plan to do with their vehicle. That's why I recommend a 90-day strategy that revolves around a pre-inspection appointment? Customers will see more value and may respond better because they don't feel like they're being sold. You can then escalate the urgency of them making a decision on their vehicle as they get closer to lease end.

2. Social Media Strategy: It's not just a buzz word, folks. In fact, what you really need to be doing right now is determining how big of an investment you need to make to grow your social-media footprint, because they don't grow overnight.

Yes, listening to and engaging your customers are the major benefits of social media, but they're not the only reason you need to get social. I look at social media as an opportunity to stay connected with customers throughout the ownership cycle, influence the content they absorb, and dramatically reduce dealer defection.

3. Digital Marketing Strategy: Traditionally, we think of digital marketing as pay-per-click advertising or search engine optimization. The reality is there is so much more to consider. You must decide whether your current strategy is really working before you dump more money into a failing plan.

To do that, determine which areas on your website are attracting the most eyes and which buttons visitors are hovering over the most, and for how long. These types of insights should be major considerations when it comes times to redesign or refresh your site's design. Remember, the name of the game is lead generation.

I also recommend looking into Internet remarketing, which is a way to track all those customers who came to your site, looked around and left without taking action. And with this knowledge, you'll be able remarket your sites and products to them continuously as they surf the Internet. If you want to learn more about this, shoot me an e-mail.

Database management, social media, and digital marketing are key ingredients to a successful marketing mix. The secret is to have a strategy that creates harmony and not chaos. Too often in our business, important initiatives are treated like checklist items. Social media is one box you can't just check off and move on. You have to plug these strategies together, track, test, modify and hold all parties accountable.

18. Pay It Forward

It's a commonly held belief that success in this business comes down to people, process and profit. So why are employees always the last in line?

No matter how busy you get, waiting for the new widgets you purchased at the recent NADA Convention, looking at ways to trim expenses or adjusting your forecasts to mirror the latest J.D. Power and Associates sales predictions, the one thing I hope you also do is assess your team.

In our fast-paced world, the importance of "human capital" can sometimes get lost in the shuffle. So, let me share with you five things you can do to ensure that's not happening at your store.

Know Them: How much do you truly know about your people? What motivates them individually? What are their interests? What is their significant other's name? Does your dealership celebrate birthdays or employment milestones?

Our industry is notorious for high turnover. One reason for that, in my opinion, is employees never feel connected. Taking a few extra minutes to get to know your people could have a huge impact on the bottom line.

Grow Them: I think it's amazing that a majority of dealers across the nation are still not actively investing in skill development for their people. How many professionals at your dealership are starving for more knowledge?

There's a constant discussion taking place at dealerships about marketing, advertising and driving traffic. It's as if these organizations believe that driving traffic into their stores will cure all ills. My question to owners and general managers is: Who has the courage to admit that their sales process needs work and that all the traffic in the world won't fix their broken process? Anyone?

If you want your employees to flourish and your team to jell, they need to be in an environment that fosters that. And the only way to do achieve that is through ongoing growth.

Inspire Them: People want something or someone to believe in. They want to know that what they do isn't just for the sake of doing something. They want to be a part of something great.

If members of your team heard someone making disparaging comments about your dealership, how many of them would stand up and defend the store? How many of them would chime in with their own negative comments? Personally, I want the guys and gals on my team to be champions of the organization. I want them to be proud of where they work. And the only way to do that is to inspire your people and make them believers in what they do.

Involve Them: Another mistake dealers make is that they very rarely, if ever, ask their staff for ideas or involve them in key decisions. Their job titles shouldn't define whether or not they have good ideas or if their opinion matters.

In fact, there are a number of successful strategies that I use in dealerships across the country that were the result of brainstorm sessions with sales and management teams. Remember, involvement creates ownership, ownership creates inspiration and inspiration creates growth.

Reward Them: There seems to be a lot of confusion around the terms "spiff" and "bonus" out there. Many look down on these terms because they wonder why you'd reward people for performing jobs they are supposed to do anyway. Unfortunately, rewards beyond the standard pay-plan bonus schedule have suffered over the last couple of years. It's time to stop squeezing the juice out of the proverbial orange and start rewarding our people.

One of the best ideas I've heard for providing employee incentives came from a dealer in Texas. He purchased everything he could on his American Express card and redeemed the rewards points to offer prizes to his sales team for hitting goals and benchmarks. He even used his points to surprise employees on their birthdays or anniversaries. He's cultivating inspired, motivated and rewarded employees without spending a dime.

Remember, employees are simply looking for autonomy, mastery and purpose, or what I call Motivation 3.0. So, if you want to drive sales and profitability higher, don't just look at your technology or advertising strategies. Look at your people strategy!

19. It's OK to 'Think Different'

F&I's resident sales expert delves into the two most important topics relevant to developing and retaining fresh talent.

It's as if Marshall Goldsmith, famed leadership development guru, read my mind when he titled his best seller, "What Got You Here Won't Get You There." We agree that, to excel in today's constantly changing marketplace, you're going to need to change things up. Strategies must be reworked. The status quo must be challenged.

Are you up to it? Do you have the stomach to rethink the way it's always been done? The good news is that I'm here to help. Picking up where we left off last month, let's look at two more areas where the status quo needs to be challenged to develop and retain fresh talent.

Training and Development

"Training" is a four-letter word to some and misunderstood by many more. To be effective, your training providers must go beyond factory test taking and shadowing a veteran salesperson for a week. Recently, a dealer remarked that she wanted to wait to see how many of the seven salespeople she hired would survive the first two weeks before determining which ones would be sent to training. Yeah, pretty amazing, right?

People, there are plenty of sound, fundamentals-based training programs on the market, many of which will never see the inside of her dealership and many others. Why? Forget the multitude of nonsensical reasons. The fact is that decision makers (and not only dealers) just don't believe in third-party training programs and don't have the leadership skills to implement or execute their own.

To paraphrase what famed management expert Peter Drucker once said, decisions are made solely by those who are empowered to make them — not by the smartest or most qualified person, just the person who can.

Another former client of mine was having trouble finding a quality F&I manager. He had gone through several hires over a couple of months. He had concerns about the "business practices" of the past F&I managers and wanted someone to do it the way he believed would best serve customers.

To help, I identified one of their salespeople with a financial background, strong CSI and a good sales track record. I also recommended an F&I company who could train the candidate I suggested. I felt this candidate's experience doing it the dealership's way on the sales floor would transition well into the F&I office, and the training would seal the deal.

It seemed like a no-brainer. Unfortunately, management just couldn't get their arms around the idea and, to this very day, F&I managers continue to come and go.

Look, I get it. You may have had a bad experience, or the previous training program you paid for just didn't stick. Or, it could be that the last team you spent money on to train left for the competition. Whatever the case, there is absolutely no reason for you to give up on training your people.

Cleaning House

My personal philosophy and commentary on the car business has been shaped over the last seven years while traveling to and working with a diverse group of dealerships across the country — from those selling 1,000 units a month to those selling 50. And throughout that time, one thing remains constant: The smaller the dealership, the smaller margin for error.

See, large stores sometimes make decisions too quickly, while smaller dealers tend to move too slow — especially when it comes to personnel decisions. Turnover is a problem in our business, but, in my opinion, we sometimes put too much stock in loyalty.

To me, loyalty is a bonus earned when someone excels at their job and maximizes profitability for their dealership. The idea that someone needs to be carried or paid for mediocre performance in the name of loyalty is crazy to me. You either expand or become expendable; it's that simple.

The reality is that tough choices will need to be made in the coming years. Everything will need to be scrutinized, which means no topic should be off limits. More opportunities will be availed to those who want to be first rather than those who wait for someone else to try it first.

You often hear that, in today's marketplace, it's more important to dominate than compete. Do you agree? If you answered "Yes," I can say with certainty that domination will never be achieved if you color inside the lines and wait for the other person to show you theirs first.

20. Challenging the Status Quo

Does life in the car business really mean working 'bell to bell'? Is good talent really that difficult to find? Sales columnist offers Part One of his take on how to fix one of the industry's biggest problems.

During a recent interview for The Norm Jones Show, a talk radio show in Detroit, I was asked what I thought was the biggest challenge facing the car business. Without hesitation, I said the inability to acquire, properly develop and retain fresh talent would prove to be an epidemic for the car business.

I have a dealer client whom I've worked with for six years, and I began to notice some blasts from the past during my last eight visits. There was the recycled sales manager, the twice-fired salespeople and a fresh-from-rehab finance manager on his third tour at the dealership. When I asked why this was happening, the client said, "It's hard to find people."

That answer, along with "This is the car business," is two of the all-too-familiar responses I often hear. So many things go unexamined, unaddressed and not dealt with in the name of our industry's culture. So, how do we change this?

What's needed to attract and retain talent in the car business? Well, let's take a look at two possible solutions.

Problem 1: The Work Schedule

The typical dealership schedule has been enforced, accepted and treated as gospel for decades. The problem is that's exactly what's kept a lot of talented people with great potential from getting into the business. It also has contributed to years of missed soccer games, vacations, family outings and countless other pursuits.

Is the bell-to-bell lifestyle the only way to successfully run a car dealership? Is the end-of-the-month frenzy to roll more vehicles and get deals done the only option for maximizing sales?

One of the first stores I worked for when I started my career offered 9 a.m. to 3 p.m. and 3 p.m. to 9 p.m. schedules. The dealership also allowed employees to take two Saturdays off per month, something that is unheard of in the car business. But why is that? Why is taking a hard look at dealership hours and work schedules so "outside the box," especially since the people making the schedule don't actually work it?

Holiday store hours are always an interesting conversation as well. I mean, how many cars can a dealership really sell over a holiday? When I ask dealers that, which I often do, the answer is usually two or three. If that's the case at your store, wouldn't you foster more goodwill among your employees by giving them the day off instead? Hey, it's just a thought.

Problem No. 2: Managers vs. Leaders

There are probably people out there more qualified than I to address leadership. However, my experience working for and with managers who never led and don't know how to lead provides me with a nice perspective on what a leader should be.

Please allow me to offer a few nuggets of advice: First, as leadership guru John Maxwell points out, good leaders are self-improving. They realize that their team must first improve themselves before improvement in performance can be realized. Yet, so many managers obtain their title and simply put the shifter into park. Leaders have subordinates by default, but what they really do is manifest followers. Managers simply have subordinates.

Let's review a few typical character differences between leaders and managers:

- An approach of calculated change vs. stability.

- Vision vs. objectives.

- Personal charisma vs. formal authority.

- Energy of passion, rather than control.

So, which traits describe you? Want to take it a step further? Put those traits on a piece of paper and ask your staff to circle options that best match you and let them anonymously provide you the results.

See, leaders create a culture of achievement that shapes outcomes. They are not focused on being right and simply producing results.

Next month, I will use this space to explore the topics of training and development. I will also address the two biggest breakthrough topics most relevant to the future. So, stay tuned.

"The question you must ask of any
TEACHER is WHEN WAS
THE LAST TIME THEY WERE A
STUDENT"

— CORY MOSLEY

21. No Training, No Complaining

By the title of this column, you might assume that my message this month is directed at sales professionals, but it isn't. What I want to do is drive home that message to those of you in decision making roles, those of you in control of the information that flows to the employees on the frontlines of your stores.

Steve Jobs, Apple's iconic founder, has an interesting quote that I often repeat when working with dealership decision makers. He said: "You cannot mandate productivity; you can only create a conducive environment where people can excel." Unfortunately, this often is not the case.

It seems like many dealers spend a ton of time on the "what" and not nearly enough time on the "how." These individuals use every meeting to hammer home the message that the dealership needs to sell more cars, conduct more customer follow-ups, and mine the customer database. Typically, the meetings end with them shouting, "Everyone needs more appointments for Saturday." Unfortunately, that's not going to get it done.

I speak to sales professionals daily. Some are past clients while others are longtime friends from my days on the sales floor. All of them seem to be telling the same old stories. So, I'd like to announce a new rule for you decision makers out there: If you don't train, then you can't complain about how slow business is, how you can't find and keep good salespeople, how everybody seems to be giving cars away, and how frustrated you are about management refusing to use the new system correctly.

Training isn't just about drills or word-tracks; it's about process, procedure, creating a great culture, improving teamwork and leading the way. If your store isn't producing at its potential, ask yourself: What new skills have you, as a decision maker, given to your team to help them be more successful?

I'm not talking about daily training sessions that recycle techniques from 30 years ago, nor am I talking about buying some new technology product or service to improve business. I want you to encourage you to be progressive and understand the human factor. Let me explain:

Expand or Become Expendable: It is my opinion that tough decisions will need to be made in the coming years, as the competition and flow of information increases and the attack on gross profit continues. I mean, how can we possibly do the same things today that we did 30 years ago?

Not long ago, I was told by a dealer that I was the first person in 11 years to conduct training at his dealership. Amazing, right? I mean, think about this: How much of that information you've learned about today's customer or that new software solution actually trickles down to the sales team? An even better question is: How hard do you push to inject new ideas into the mix or encourage your people to take a fresh look at the way your store conducts business?

Say Hello to Gen Y: My guess is most of the people making up your sales team are in the dark about those customers who were born between 1981 and 1994. It's unfortunate if that's the case, because that market is 75 million customers strong. This is a generation that is four times more likely to respond to text messages than voicemails, and currently accounts for 25 percent of all car buyers. Most experts believe that percentage will increase to 40 percent in the next 10 years.

Now, those stats only skim the surface as to what motivates this generation. One thing you can be certain about is word-tracks such as, "What would it take to earn your business?" and "If I could, would you?" aren't going to work on this generation.

It's time to move forward, folks. It's no longer about whether your team is good or bad; it's about how we can get better. See, as the challenges become more sophisticated, so do the strategies needed to ensure continued success. The good news is most problems can be attributed to a deficiency of knowledge, which can be corrected fairly quickly. And with the right long-term plan of action, it can be cured forever.

As a decision maker in a dealership, you control what information gets disseminated to the sales pros on the frontlines. So, I would ask that you make an effort to seek out a fresh perspective and treat your mind like an umbrella, which, as you know, works best when it's open.

22. Momentum: Getting It and Keeping It

The excitement that comes when things click on an individual and business level is indescribable. There are plenty of customers on the lot, tons of Internet leads flowing and customers and banks saying, "Let's do the deal!" We in the car business like to refer to that as "good times."

I laid out four potential game-changers that, if implemented, can ensure increased success for your retail operations. By definition, momentum cannot be achieved without motion. To put things in motion, a foundation must be laid first. So, let's fire up the cement mixer and start pouring.

- **Identify one idea, process or strategy that must be changed:** One reason many of us never get around to changing things is that the challenges appear too great and we don't know where to begin. If you start with one item at a time, you can significantly increase your chances of making a complete change. When I take on a turnaround project at a dealership, I use this same strategy. The little changes add up, and the snowball effect begins to create momentum.

- **Ask a respected colleague how they do things:** The ego can be a dangerous thing. Unwillingness to seek advice keeps some really talented people from getting to the next level. If you are the top guy at your dealership, make it your responsibility to mentor a new sales professional. If you're looking for answers, seek out people who are operating at the level to which you aspire. Come up with some intelligent questions, track them down and ask away. This is how you'll become a better salesperson, manager, GM or even dealer. If you are in senior management, join a 20 Group. If you are a sales professional, seek out a professional network for auto sales people. If you can't find one, let me know.

- **Put a new issue on the table:** Sometimes the breakthrough comes from the things you don't see or think about normally, like an untouchable process, employee, vendor or ritual.

- **Re-establish your goals:** Goals usually range from sales, gross and income. They can be determined by you, your manager, dealer or, best of all — insert sarcastic smirk here — the manufacturer. Don't be afraid to adjust your goals. ... And I don't mean lower. Instead, recommit yourself and, while you're at it, think even bigger!

- **Review your 'Why':** What's the mission? Why are you doing what you're doing the way you're doing it? We can forget about the spiritual awakening for now and just keep this idea focused on your career.

- **Rally the troops:** If you are in management, get everyone involved by spreading the word about fresh ideas, new goals and a renewed approach. Leverage energy and these new ideas to accelerate momentum. If you are flying solo, tell someone about your new changes and the new outcomes you are going to attain. Tell the guy or gal in the desk next to you, Tweet about it or tell all your Facebook friends — and be accountable.

- **Start taking positive action:** "Action" is a word that's often referenced but rarely realized, usually because it involves work. Business guru Jim Rohn once said, "What is easy to do is also easy not to do." In a sense, this makes doing nothing a form of action; it's just the wrong kind. Amongst the many nuggets of wisdom that were imparted to me by my barber as a teenager, the phrase "Don't talk about it, be about it," was one of the greatest.

The truth is we need momentum. It calls for energy, drives belief in things to come and can make people fearless. It can drive you to make that extra call, take that extra "up" and refuse to give up the gross when a customer counters your numbers. Momentum keeps the competitive spirit alive in the store. You need it, I need it and the dealership must have it to dominate.

The path to the next level requires creative thinking, the courage to change and the courage to try something you've never done before. The spirit of the car business is alive and is ready to reward those willing to step up to the plate and get it done. I challenge myself every day and now I will challenge you: E-mail me and let me know what actions you are going to take today. I'll follow up with you in 30 days to see how it's going.

23. Four Operational Game-Changers

I have worked with a lot of talented people in this business, many of whom went on to be key leaders within their organizations. Recent conversations with some of those individuals and the completion of an important project inspired me to write this month's column. You may not like what I have to say, but, hopefully, it will act as a catalyst for change.

See, in today's marketplace, "little by little" isn't the answer. Neither is "moving at a glacial pace." Reaching a dominant position requires massive action. The following are the first four of nine ideas that, if successfully implemented, will create the momentum you need to do just that:

Get feedback from your sales team: At my company, we offer something called "Breakthrough Consulting." It's designed to identify the major roadblocks preventing a dealership from reaching the next level. First, I gather the sales team alone in a room. With no managers present, they are free to tell me what's really happening at the dealership. It also allows me to extract their ideas for getting increased results.

I started in the showroom myself, and I've been consulting long enough to know the difference between complaints and actual challenges. The truth is that some of the best ideas for moving the sales department forward rest in the minds of your sales team. Unfortunately, many great ideas for inventory, pricing, pay plans, incentive plans, marketing and even cost cutting fall on deaf ears because the decision maker is too ego-driven to accept recommendations from their subordinates.

Remember, successful salespeople are good for more than just writing deals and mastering the meet and greet. Most of them have creative ideas that are not solely focused on increasing their income. In fact, many sales professionals simply want to have a role in the dealership's success. So, why not start weekly meetings to discuss new ideas or create a process by which ideas can be submitted for serious consideration?

Get rid of the sacred cows: I've written it before and I'll write it again: Expand or become expendable. If my 66-year-old mother is texting, e-mailing, Face booking and tweeting, then there is no excuse for salespeople and managers not being able to do the same. Properly using the CRM system or surfing the Web to educate yourself on the information your customers are finding online should be a daily job requirement.

I can't tell you how many times I've seen capable sales, finance and service managers — including sales professionals — sink a dealership. Decision makers need to look in the mirror and be honest, because it's critical that they put more energy into those who are committed to enhancing the business rather than those who simply will not step up.

Sweep away the bureaucracy: Just like the sacred cows, the bureaucracy and red tape has got to go. "Nimble," "quick" and "responsive" need to become the new adjectives in your life, as death by meeting and paralysis by analysis will kill even the best of intentions.

To increase the level of communication across the dealership, the "us vs. them" mentality that manifests in the sales, finance and service departments must be eliminated. And don't just talk about an open-door policy; literally unscrew the doors from their hinges, reengage your passion for the business and reignite that fire within your sales and management teams.

Don't recycle talent: I'm all for recycling when it comes to bottles, cans and paper, but not when it comes to employees. One of my clients has a manager on his fourth tour at the dealership. He was fired at the end of the three previous go-arounds. Do yourself a favor and don't make the same mistake.

I've often said that the length of your tenure in the business has no bearing on how competent and skilled you are. You read right — none! I've met second-year managers who could run circles around the so-called veterans. And by utilizing personality profiling, tweaking the pay plan and work schedule, and participating in a real training and development program, you too will be able to attract and retain the talent that you'll need to dominate in the future.

24. Seven Team-Building Must-Haves

The coaching and development of sales staff always sounds like the right thing to do, but very rarely is it done consistently and, more importantly, properly. Many times, we assume the best person for the job is the one with a manager's title. Unfortunately, that's not always the case.

Take a recent conversation I had with a sales manager. He remarked to me that one of his salespeople was on thin ice because he wasn't closing his customers. I asked about his store's training program. "We don't have a formal training program," he responded, adding that he personally shadows his salespeople and that his experience in the real-estate business served as the only reference his team needed.

Apparently, poorly performing salespeople are supposed to miraculously get better at their jobs. I asked the manager if he could coach his salespeople. "I don't have time," he said, which I took to mean he didn't know how.

See, according to Dr. John C. Hall and John Steuermol — innovators in the field of selection testing — there are seven critical components to becoming a great coach. Let's examine each one and see if we can turn you into the coach your dealership and your team needs.

1. Be your own ally: The primary focus here is to instill in your sales team a positive and optimistic outlook. You want to keep them from playing mental games against each other and fostering negativity that impedes performance. So, rather than starting another Saturday sales meeting by telling your staff how much they suck, think of a positive way to motivate them to victory.

2. Maximize your return on energy: Coach your sales team to avoid common distractions and unproductive activities, such as coffee klatches, during high ROI times of the day. It is so easy to misuse your time when you work the car schedule, so be sure to provide your team with a game plan for winning the day.

3. Prospect: This is a great opportunity to share and exchange strategies on how to prospect both inside and outside the dealership.

4. Develop a compelling story: Help your team develop sales approaches that speak to the needs of your store's most common type of clients. All customers are not the same, so why should the sales approach be?

5. Become a master of communication: The core focus here is to help your sales team communicate the brand and dealership's message effectively. Identify and reinforce particular components of your store's sales message that add the most value.

6. Sharpen the saw: Although it's sad to say, the idea of continuous learning among sales professionals is very rarely taken seriously. I've been in dealerships all over the country, including some of the largest dealership groups, and can only recall one that had a recommended reading list for ongoing improvement. That dealership also provided spiffs to encourage team members to read and advance their skills. It's no wonder the store boasted the highest grosses in its area.

7. Keeping Score: Show me a salesperson who doesn't want to win, and I'll show you one who isn't making money or hitting their sales objectives. Top performers, who really care about what they do want to know that they are crushing it, so track and monitor your salespeople regularly and encourage them along the way.

We have more technology and widgets at our disposal than ever before, but so does the competition. That's why your employees remain a critical factor in differentiating your store from your competitors, so be sure to utilize and develop that talent. Change your approach and see what happens. I promise you won't be disappointed.

"CREDIBILITY
when they call you up
and just say
WHERE DO I SIGN?"

—————————— - CORY MOSLEY

III. Dealer Principal

25. Out with the Old

Even before the recession took hold of our industry, the Internet was changing the game for auto dealers. I'm sure you've seen the stat from J.D. Power and Associates: Eighty percent of car shoppers do research online before they ever enter a dealership. There are some other stats to consider as well.

According to CNW Research, Internet prospects in 2009 generated an average gross profit of $754 — the lowest figure for any customer type. And that's for the customers who bought cars, as the average closing ratio for Internet prospects was a woeful 18.1 percent in the first quarter of last year.

I blame these numbers on a difficult-to-break connection between the fundamentals of successful selling and the ideas that are considered "old school." The meet-and-greet and test drive are considered indispensable tools of the sales process. Then there are the old-school word-tracks and catchphrases, such as "Come on down," and "Help me help you." The problem with lines like that is the way we need to communicate with customers has changed.

As I touched on earlier, the Internet is forcing this change. Easy access to more dealers and more information will continue to raise customers' level of education. The challenge we face is that many salespeople and managers do not invest their time to understand the type of information their customers are exposed to. The ability to provide third-party credibility has become a key element to increasing closing ratios and maintaining favorable gross profit.

Let's look at four key areas that, if improved, will help you meet the particular challenges of the new-school customer.

1. Expand Your Online Education

Invest whatever time you can in poring over the latest third-party data on the cars you sell. Start with Edmunds.com and KBB.com. Also check out newer sites like TrueCar.com. These three and many others wield a great deal of power with today's consumer, so it's important to be able to "talk the talk" with this new-school customer.

2. Get More Training

Seek out training that improves your communication. Training is not the act of learning something one time; training is conditioning. LeBron James has known how to shoot a basketball for a long time, but the conditioning and repetition of doing it is what made him great. So, your challenge will be to expose yourself to new information and start to replace some of the old-school word-tracks and techniques with new ones.

3. Step Outside of Your Box

Work on modeling your prospects. This basically means mirroring their tone and body language. It also means listening for ways to make a connection. It's highly likely that you're doing a great job selling to customers with whom you connect on a personal level. The disconnect between dealer and customer typically occurs when there is a personality mismatch. When that happens, it's easy to go from conversational to confrontational.

4. Reevaluate Your Methods

A quick, easy, but powerful way to evaluate your sales methods is to simply write down what you're doing now and why you do it that way. Once you've done that, ask yourself if there is a better way. Yes, a breakthrough can be that simple to attain.

Your mission is to master the ability to achieve incremental sales. Think about the impact four to seven extra deals per salesperson per month would have on your store's income and business profitability? So, get started, get ready, and let the summer selling season begin. I plan to be with you along your journey and I look forward to helping you increase your results — no matter what your job title is.

26. Winning Online

I'm often asked at dealerships, seminars and 20 Group meetings what is the key element of success for selling cars online. My answer is always the same: First and foremost, the dealer principal must take an active role in making sure e-success happens. That means going beyond stated intentions and actively supporting the Internet department.

I've found that dealers with successful, profit-driving Internet sales departments have five things in common. Let's take a closer look at each one:

They invest in the proper technology: These dealers use the same due diligence in choosing Internet-related products and services as they do when buying products and services for fixed operations.

They emphasize return on investment more than expense: These statements should sound familiar: "These leads are expensive," "Maintaining this website is too expensive," and "Customer relationship management software is way too expensive." A dealer principal or primary decision-maker must realize that cutting corners isn't always cost effective. In fact, cutting corners can actually cost money in front- and back-end gross, F&I income and service business.

Their opinions of Internet buyers are based on research rather than opinion: These statements may also sound familiar: "Low gross," "Looking to steal cars," and "Not serious buyers." Those statements represent how many dealers view online shoppers. If you don't see the value, then your actions to attract Internet buyers won't be effective. This also applies to decision-makers who don't verbalize their negative feelings.

They invest in training Internet personnel: Internet staff or personnel manning the business development center are arguably the most undertrained people in the dealership today. Many staffers are assigned to the Internet department simply because they know how to send and receive e-mails. It is irrational to put untrained employees on the frontlines to face hundreds of potential customers a month. How can you rationalize spending thousands of dollars a month for leads, CRM software and a website, but not spend anything on training? What message are you sending to an Internet professional starving for support?

They understand the value of metrics and accountability: Expected results can and should be measured. Stop going with your gut and use those measurements when selecting lead providers and website vendors. Also use that data when deciding who will man your Internet department.

If you feel you have the basics covered, here are three power tips to energize your Internet department:

- Brainstorm with experienced people: Would you readily take parenting advice from someone who isn't a parent? So why discuss Internet strategy with colleagues lacking strategic Internet experience?

- Recognize that technology isn't a silver bullet: All technology is created by people. Technology also can be utilized effectively or ineffectively by people.

- Train, train, train: Albert Einstein said the definition of insanity is doing the same thing over and over again and expecting different results. How do you move the needle in your dealership if your employees are using poor or, worse, undefined techniques, processes or follow-up action plans? An investment in training is an investment in improving results.

The best thing any dealer principal or decision-maker can do is get involved in the educational process. They should also be involved in determining where the department is, where it needs to go and how. They also need to be involved in the execution of the plan.

Success online this year will depend on the same things that drive the showroom: people, processes and technology. Yes, I know the tech part is a moving target, so properly vet your providers, talk to other dealers and don't be afraid to get multiple opinions regarding your next steps.

There is no logical reason why the dealer down the street should be burning it up online while your Internet department is stuck in neutral. So, ask yourself: "Am I the one standing in the way of my dealership's online success?" If the answer is "Yes," get out of the way and into the game.

27. Top Priorities

I asked a few industry experts and friends to dust off their crystal balls and share their thoughts, advice and predictions for the automotive marketplace. We all agree that change is always in the air, so let's see what new technology, processes and strategies will top the list of priorities for your dealership this year.

Jeff Clark, DealerON

Savvy dealers are going to be putting more time and resources toward marketing fixed-operations online. For the typical dealer, service makes up more than 50 percent of their gross profit, yet they only devote a handful of pages on their website to that department. Here are three ways to change that:

• Create high volumes of pages of parts and service content designed to compete for organic search traffic.

• Utilize different primary lead forms (online appointment schedulers, phone numbers in large fonts and printable coupons).

• Be more direct with your website's calls to action ("Schedule," "Call" and "Print" rather than "Click," "Submit" or "Email").

Also make sure that your service department content is mobile-enabled and optimized. Mobile devices now represent anywhere from 12 to 20 percent of a dealership's website traffic and the service appointment pages have an even higher mix of mobile traffic than that. So, make sure it's easy to schedule an appointment and locate phone numbers, and be sure to have a click-to-call feature.

Paul Potratz, Potratz Partners Advertising

Dealers looking to be high performers should shift their focus to three crucial areas: mobile marketing, content engagement and social media marketing.

• Mobile Marketing: Fifty percent of car shoppers are connected to a smart phone. It's also one of the first tools they use when they begin their shopping process, so what better way to reach them? Dealers should also keep an eye on mobile apps, text and social game marketing.

• Content Engagement: If you are not discussing engagement percentages and averages, shopping cart abandonment rates and return cycles, you are missing a lot of opportunities. It's not a question of how to drive more leads; it's how quickly you convert the traffic.

• Social Media Marketing: Hiring an outside company to manage 100 percent of your campaigns is a waste of time and money. You need to have a social media director, a position which can be outsourced. You also need buy-in from your dealer and key employees.

Todd Smith, ActivEngage

Traditional advertising is giving way to inbound marketing, which relies on putting your dealership in a position to be found by search engines and other means. It's a powerful way to reduce cost per vehicle sold while ensuring their marketing message is in the right place at the right time.

I believe more dealers will begin to put conversion techniques in place for their social media marketing. I foresee a host of new apps and tools coming into the marketplace that will allow dealerships to turn social-media window shoppers into active buyers.

Dealers also will continue to demand better business intelligence.

Raj Sundaram, DealerTrack

Mobile technology continues to redefine how dealerships operate. Dealers demand control, flexibility and access to their vehicle, customer, and transaction information across their entire dealership. Open technology enables that through secure, real-time and seamless integration between all systems running within a dealership.

The increased focus and investment in digital retailing is forcing every dealer to focus on developing user-friendly websites that have rich and timely content. Dealers are succeeding in turning inventory faster and more profitably if their sites have high quality pictures, video and impactful descriptions. The push will be to link payments and financing to inventory.

Dealers must also embrace a commitment to develop their people through training, team building and adding tools to make sales teams more effective. Progress is a process, so let's get started.

28. Calling All Business Managers

The Internet era is definitely challenging the F&I office these days, but that doesn't mean there aren't other opportunities to drive profitability. The magazine's dealership strategist weighs in.

I recently heard the 1980s classic, "Don't You (Forget About Me)," by Simple Minds. The song was being used in a TV promo for a returning show on the USA Network. It got me thinking about the always-entertaining relationship between the sales department and the F&I office.

The major ongoing issue, as you all know, centers on how sales departments consistently put together deals that have no regard for F&I profitability. No doubt we could have a lengthy discussion over that issue, especially as the sales process continues to migrate online. So, rather than have a debate neither side will win, I'd like to focus on a couple of things F&I offices can do to maintain profitability after the customer takes delivery of the vehicle.

Yes, the name of the game is to get the customer to agree to a product at the time of purchase. However, with the exception of products like GAP, which has to be included in the deal at the time of purchase, there are several other products that can generate incremental gross profit in F&I. All it takes is a little post-sale marketing. Let's take a look:

Extended Warranties and Service Contracts: In most cases, a customer has the option to purchase a service contract up until the expiration of his or her factory warranty, which means you have a good three-plus years to sell an extension or VSC. So, does your dealership have a marketing strategy to promote those products via e-mail, "snail" mail, text or phone? Is there an offer available that would motivate a customer to purchase a service agreement? Are you checking service repair orders to identify customers whose factory warranties are about to expire? If not, you're missing a great opportunity to market those products.

Aftermarket Accessories: It's amazing that an industry based on car buyers wanting to express themselves by customizing their vehicles is worth $28 billion a year. It's even more amazing that car dealers are only cashing in on 5.3 percent of that market. One reason may be that customers typically add accessories to their vehicles six months or more after taking delivery. Maybe they need to save a little money before pulling the trigger, or maybe that's how long it takes for them to realize their vehicle looks similar to thousands of others on the road. Whichever the case, you must identify your accessory touch points to capitalize.

Service Plans: Have you considered developing and deploying your own prepaid maintenance plan? These programs represent an additional revenue stream, and they provide a firm guarantee that you won't send your service department's bread-and-butter business to the local Jiffy Lube.

New Products for Old Customers:

As you work to expand your product lineup and services in the finance office, don't neglect products and services that don't need to be purchased at the point of sale. Remember, the name of the game is incremental gains. There are plenty of good products available that will help you market to your past customers. I know it sounds overly simplistic, but I also know how difficult it can be to implement a strategy that can pay dividends further down the line in a sell-it-now dealership environment.

But how great would it be to know that, based on your efforts, you can eventually realize an extra two to four service contracts, one or two accessory sales, a couple of PPMs and, just for kicks, the sale of that new vehicle-recovery system you brought in? I always love opportunities that don't force the store to reinvent the wheel to pick up a few extra dollars. So get started, get going and get it done!

29. 'On the Point'

How did you do last year? Did you accomplish everything you set out to do this year? Did you fulfill your promises of financial success? More importantly, in the face of all the bad news on the airwaves these days, were you able to stay focused on your economy rather than the economy?

As the old cliché goes, hindsight is 20/20. So, the question should really be: What would you have done differently? The best thing about life is that every new day presents a new opportunity to take action. If you're focused on continuous education, then every day presents an opportunity to take greater action.

Let me share a personal story with you. Fresh from an onsite training class I gave one rainy morning in Texas, I saw two salesmen standing outside on the point. The rain began to subside, so I walked over and stood between the two gentlemen to get into the conversation.

The salesman to my left started lamenting that the rain was killing business and it was a waste of time to be at the dealership. The salesman to my right called the other guy's comment "crazy," arguing that customers who visit on rainy days are the best buyers. He then said he couldn't wait for the next customer to walk onto the lot.

So, there I stood between two colleagues with the same opportunities, same business cards, and the same desks in the same showroom, both trying to sell the same inventory based on the same pay plan. Now, the guy to my left just happened to be the lowest man on the dealership's totem pole. The guy to my right was the top salesperson at the dealership, appearing atop the leader board on a regular basis.

See, it's not necessarily skill level that separates the good from the bad; it's attitude. And, as the saying goes, your attitude determines your altitude. Let's take a look at three intangible qualities that separated those two salesmen and how a renewed focus on each can help keep you on the point:

1. Hunger: The top guy was hungry, wouldn't you agree? Think about it: Hungry people don't walk at the bell, ask about the lunch order at 10:30 a.m. or participate in the daily coffee klatch. You won't hear them complaining about the advertising or the leasing programs. Hungry people aren't concerned about who's getting house deals and why. Instead, they are focused on ways to maximize their pay plans.

Hungry individuals assume everyone is a buyer until they find out otherwise. Hungry people always have a suggestion on how to make the deal work. They aren't scared of customers who walk in with their Internet research, and they are always ready to put a deal together. Hungry sales-people complete their work plan every day, set personal goals and work toward them. These are people who think win-win for the customer, themselves and the dealership.

2. Action: Success also finds people who take action. Those who take action are more effective because they try harder, keep things in motion, accomplish more in less time and are willing to take a shot. These individuals keep going until the deal is done or dead, and apply energy toward learning from missed opportunities.

3. Having the Right Focus: Lastly, success finds people who focus not only on what they know, but on what they can actually do. Every time I speak at a conference, there's always one guy in the audience who will come up to me after my presentation and tell me that the presenter before me offered the same advice. My response is always the same: "That's great, so how good are you at executing on it?" I usually hear the same excuses in return: They either forgot to use the technique, or they have a better method — even though they never seem to have the gross numbers to back it up.

See, it's never about whether you know something or not; it's about how good you are at it. When you take the time to focus on what you are doing, it's easier for you to identify the things that may be standing in your way. As Confucius once said, "By nature, men are nearly alike; by practice they get to be wide apart."

"Although there are many ways to simply

SELL MORE

INCREMENTAL AND SUSTAINABLE GROWTH is

THE RIGHT WAY!"

— CORY MOSLEY

30. To BDC or Not to BDC

I've been involved with departments framed around the business development center name since 1999. Funny thing is, some of the same questions that came up back then still persist today:

"Do I need a BDC?"

"What should a BDC do?"

"How should people in the BDC be paid?"

(And my favorite): "What's the difference between a BDC and an Internet department?"

I always smile when I hear someone at a dealership tell me, "We don't have a BDC, we have a CDC." For those who haven't heard of that acronym before, it stands for customer development center. Another variation is customer retention center or CRC. The truth is the goals are the same regardless of the label you attach to that department.

Now, there are experts out there preaching the certain demise of the BDC. They are telling dealers they need to become an Internet dealership. The belief is that, through the dealership's CRM solution, every salesperson can be their customers' Captain America. It sounds good in theory, but adopting that belief is more abstract than practical for a majority of today's dealerships.

Let me be clear: I'm not talking about the small percentage of stores that have successfully gone the route of the Internet dealership. But why did we create a BDC or Internet department in the first place? Did it have to do with the theory that salespeople aren't good at following up with customers, as their main focus is on the bird in the hand (i.e., in-store customer)? Did we do it because we wanted to maximize all revenue streams and just allow salespeople to do, at least theoretically, what they do best? It's probably a bit of all of the above.

I'm always amazed at how industry pundits prophesize about the future of the dealership environment. That's because after visiting hundreds of dealerships and with thousands of dealership personnel, I have yet to find a store that doesn't have trouble implementing the fundamentals on a daily basis, let alone investing in the education required to serve the future Gen-Y buyer.

Take this story I caught wind of a few months ago: A salesperson was sent into early retirement because of a simple mandate the dealership put forth. What was it? Well, all management wanted was for salespeople to contact customers on their birthdays. Talk about a dealership in need of a BDC.

Now, let's look at the typical tasks of a BDC:

- Handle incoming sales calls.

- Follow up with unsold showroom customers.

- Be responsible for equity and other promotional calls.

- Administer targeted e-mail campaigns and e-newsletters.

- Build fleet business.

- Handle lease returns and renewals, including all related phone, mail and e-mail communications.

- Handle Internet leads and appointment setting.

- Conduct parts and service retention marketing.

- Conduct internal CSI calls and e-mails.

- Resolve all parts and service-related issues within pre-determined parameters.

- Monitor and manage dealer reputation issues.

- Turn over deals that involve Internet customers.

- Provide updated market pricing data to management and staff.

- Should I go on? Now, here are a couple of reasons a BDC fails:

- It wasn't staffed correctly.

- Functions and desired outcomes were never properly defined.

- You deem the job as entry level, pay entry-level wages and hire entry-level talent.

- No one on the BDC staff is empowered.

- There is little to no investment in training.

- Success hinges on one person.

Whether you have a roomful of people and call them your dealership's BDC or not, you will need people who are capable of executing a sophisticated, business-generating and customer-retention plan. To achieve that, you need to ask yourself two important questions: 1) How much change am I open to? and 2) How far am I willing to go to push my employees?

Answers to those questions must factor in the culture of the store and the style in which the store is run. So, to BDC or not to BDC ... Is that really the question?

31. No Traffic on the Extra Mile

Many of you may be thinking that the landscape is very different today compared to a few years ago, but, according to the National Automobile Dealers Association, the average gross profit on a new car over the last 10 years is down by $227. That's $34 per deal on a 15 percent commission plan. I bet that isn't as much as you thought, and it is certainly a figure you can surpass.

Now, we're all familiar with the line, "There's no business like show business." Well, I wouldn't personally know if that's true or not, but I can say from firsthand experience that there is no business like the car business — not just for the controversy and characters, but for the triumphs as well.

In the car business, you have a group of people that range from the dealer principal to the lot attendant, who earns a living and gets some satisfaction from a job well done. On the sales side, you have an environment where guys and gals from all backgrounds spend a lot of time trying to sell one more car, make a few more dollars, hit the next bonus level and, in some cases, produce enough for a particular month to have the opportunity to do it all over again.

I recently read an article about pay plans for sales professionals. It detailed changes some dealers are making to their plans to help retain talent and, ultimately, make it worthwhile for someone to put in the work. My question to you is: What are you doing to improve your own bottom line without depending on new bonus plans or blockbuster advertising?

If you have been in the car business for any amount of time, I bet I can summarize your career thus far: When you started, you were probably like me — ready to take on the world. You were determined to be the best, standing tall on the point and waiting for that next "up." Or, you were positioned next to the phone, ready to grab that next "phone up." Unfortunately, things changed. Time, life and the daily lunch decisions sucked some of the fire out of you. Now here you are with however many years on the job, still trying to make it happen. But are you still trying hard enough?

One of the things that I believe makes me a great dealership strategist is my ability to approach a project with a short-term view. This means I have to figure out the problem and the fix quickly. I only have a certain number of weeks or months to come up with a solution. This gift can also be a curse, because my transient nature spills over into my personal life.

As a car customer, I prefer short-term leases of 24 months and will take a maximum of 30 months. What does this mean to you? Well, every year, for at least the last five years, I have played the role of customer in search of a vehicle and, more importantly, a great sales experience. The problem is I'm still searching for that experience.

Now, for the record, I know plenty of fantastic salespeople all over the country. However, because I don't purchase vehicles from clients, there is no bias in my approach.

In the last six months, I visited Subaru, BMW, Mercedes-Benz, Land Rover, Infiniti and Lexus dealerships. I received only one professional vehicle presentation, and almost zero follow-up from these dealerships. This is despite each store having some fancy customer relationship management program. How can this be? A wise man I know said that anyone who doesn't work to get better in today's market will be punished by that market and the increasing options, demands and changing attitudes of its buyers.

Take control of your own outcome. Don't wait for anyone and don't blame anyone. Here a seven keys to breaking away from the pack:

1. Learn what others won't take the time to learn.

2. Study others who are more successful than you are.

3. Seek out more opportunities. (You can't imagine the number of people who run from Internet customers, retention customers or orphan owners.)

4. Work on delivering more service and value than you are getting paid for.

5. Don't walk, but run from the daily coffee klatch.

6. Stay in your lane and focus on your book of business.

7. Dig deep into your pocket and pay for your education. It will come back to you tenfold.

As the headline says, there is no traffic on the extra mile, only profit and opportunity. You are, of course, greatly encouraged to give it your all and try to prove me wrong!

About the Author

Once named the 'Hardest Workin' Man in the Automotive Training & Consulting Business,' Cory is a nationally recognized authority in the areas of progressive retail strategy, e-commerce sales & marketing, and technology-assisted selling.

Cory has worked with some of the most recognized names in the automotive industry, including mega groups and manufacturers. He lectures nationwide at events like the NADA convention and Driving Sales Executive Summit.

As a champion of the retail sales professional, Cory's strategies and selling techniques are based on the real-world selling environment and are designed to increase profits for the dealer and the 'front-line' employee.

Mosley Automotive Training Solutions
Dealer Development Program

The Dealer Development Program combines customized consulting, training and coaching into a foundational program that supports dealers' long-term goals. Our cutting-edge team stands ready to help your dealership achieve incremental and sustainable growth.

Available for an affordable monthly investment, the DDP provides access to:

- The latest marketplace trends and strategies

- Our dealer consortium, including umbrella pricing for various products and services your dealership uses

- Ongoing consulting and process development for your team

- Proven strategies for e-commerce development and customer relationship management (CRM)

Ad-Hoc Consulting & Training

Our ad-hoc consulting and training ranges from basic strategic consulting to ongoing customized training sessions. We know that one size doesn't fit all. What works for one dealer a thousand miles away may not be the right approach for your dealership. Group training is available on-site or via our e-learning platform. Our analysis includes face-to-face meetings with management and applicable personnel.

Mosley 24/7 Virtual Training

Mosley 24/7 equips your store with the most dynamic virtual training available on the market. Built and hosted on the fast and reliable Light Speed VT platform, Mosley 24/7 connects your teams to on-demand training so they can master the latest in personality, gen-y, and Internet sales strategies. Your dealership has full control to train, test and certify every sales professional in the dealership to accelerate sales and fuel profitability.

Jeffrey Gitomer Certified Training

Cory Mosley is one of the fewer than 100 people that "King of Sales" Jeffrey Gitomer has certified worldwide to present his award-winning sales strategies. Cory is certified to present these four, widely acclaimed programs:

- The Little Red Book of Selling (No. 1 selling sales book of all time)

- The Little Gold Book of YES! Attitude

- The Little Black Book of Connections

- Customer Satisfaction is Worthless, Customer Loyalty is Priceless

DiSC Profiles & Assessments

Mosley Automotive Training is an exclusive partner with Everything DiSC ®, a leading personal assessment tool used by more than 40 million people to improve work productivity, teamwork and communication. As an accredited partner, we can provide DiSC assessments to your entire dealership team with tailored assessments that include Everything DiSC Workplace and Everything DiSC Sales.

OEM/Enterprise Programs

We have developed several core programs that can be integrated into current or future business applications at the OEM and enterprise level. We specialize in delivering solutions in the current areas:

- E-commerce initiatives

- Dealership process consulting

- Curriculum development

- Program staffing, deployment and management

- Seminars and live events

- Call center solutions

Contact Information

MOSLEY AUTOMOTIVE
SALES STRATEGY AND TRAINING

Mosley Automotive
3741 Westerre Parkway
Suite B
Richmond, VA 23233
Main: 877.667.5398

Email: info@mosleytraining.com

www.mosleyautomotive.com

 mosleyautomotive

 @corymosley

 in/corymosley

28258173R00088

Made in the USA
Charleston, SC
05 April 2014